# Doing Good

# Better

# Doing Good Better

## Better

Revised and Updated

How to be an Effective Board Member
of a Nonprofit Organization

# Edgar Stoesz

Good Books

New York, New York

Good Books books may be purchased in bulk at special discounts for sales promotion, corporate gifts, fund-raising, or educational purposes. Special editions can also be created to specifications. For details, contact the Special Sales Department, Good Books, 307 West 36th Street, 11th Floor, New York, NY 10018 or info@skyhorsepublishing.com.

Good Books is an imprint of Skyhorse Publishing, Inc.®, a Delaware corporation.

Visit our website at www.goodbooks.com.

10 9 8 7 6 5 4

Library of Congress Cataloging-in-Publication Data is available on file.

Cover design by Cliff Snyder

Print ISBN: 978-1-56148-824-7
Ebook ISBN: 978-1-68099-084-3

Printed in the United States of America

# Table of Contents

## Exhibits

# Acknowledgments

"No man is an island." These classic words were penned by John Donne when he was believed to be on his death bed. I borrow them to acknowledge all the people who helped to shape my life and give it meaning. I owe much to the following persons:

My parents, Anna and Dietrich

My wife of 56 years, Gladys

My teachers, both formal and informal

My mentors who gave me an opportunity to develop and practice my talents

My co-workers who joined me as we together worked to make life better for many

My children and grandchildren who love me

As pertains to this book specifically, I acknowledge with appreciation the good work Phyllis Pellman Good did in editing my work and making it more readable. I also acknowledge the valuable role of Skyhorse Publishing in the publication and marketing of the book.

# Preface to This Revised and Updated Edition

In this little, highly readable book are my learnings from a lifetime of service in a variety of nonprofit and for-profit boards, sometimes as director, often as chair, sometimes as a CEO responsible to a board.

**Doing Good Better** is a pragmatic book, dealing with boardroom realities, enriched by what I've drawn from other scholars and practitioners. In 26 short chapters and six exhibits, the book covers the whole gamut of a board's governance responsibility, from servicing the membership to delegating board decisions to the CEO for implementation.

Nonprofits, and many other organizations, are about doing good. **Doing Good Better** is about helping them do it better and enjoy it more. May you find ideas and suggestions here that make your board work more effective.

This revised and updated edition is a complete re-write of my earlier books dating back to 1994. Readers of the earlier editions will find it a useful review, while new readers will find it to be a more complete and renewed presentation.

More than a recitation of boardroom best practices, **Doing Good Better** is infused with an *attitude* of board service. Serving on a board is seen as a privilege, and we should do it with joyful spirits. The benefits of board service accrue to the cause being served, as well as to the director. Those who are willing to serve on the board of a worthy cause are a unique and beautiful class of people who have an *other* orientation.

At the same time, board service provides an opportunity to discover and develop new skills while making lifelong friendships. It is truly in giving that we receive.

So welcome aboard. Roll up your sleeves. Join in **Doing Good Better!**

Edgar Stoesz
Fall, 2015

# CHAPTER 1

# Organizational Greatness Begins with Great People

G reat organizations begin with great people. Apart from people, an organization is only an empty shell. It knows nothing. It can do nothing. It is people that imbue an organization with greatness.

"The only way anything ever runs itself," said one successful leader, "is downhill. Trees—have you noticed?—die from the top. That is true also of organizations."

In his highly acclaimed book, *Good to Great and the Social Sectors*, Jim Collins suggests that the formula for organizational greatness is: (a) getting the right persons on the bus; (b) getting the wrong persons off the bus; and (c) positioning them on the bus for maximum effectiveness. Organizational greatness is all about people.

## Building a great board

Building a better board begins with an objective examination of your current board membership, including the following qualifications:

**Competencies:** Do you have on your board the skills needed to give direction to the organization you are directing? This includes professional skills in the field of your endeavor, financial savvy, proven leadership ability, human relations competence, and just plain common sense. What do your directors know? What can they do?

**Representation:** Is your board more or less representative of the membership/constituency? Does it include women and men, young and experienced, and persons representing your ethnic and religious diversity? When your supporters see a picture of your board, you want them to say, "We feel well represented by them."

**Proven performance:** Are there directors on your board who are not pulling their weight or whose attendance record is lacking? Harboring dead wood is not just an inert place at the table. It is a negative. It suggests that poor performance is tolerated at the highest organizational levels.

When the results of this self-analysis are known, you need to act on your findings. The Board Service Committee, an expansion of what was previously known as the Nominating Committee, usually handles this task. It is arguably the most important committee on your board since it holds the key to your future effectiveness.

> **The Nominating Committee is arguably the most important committee on a board.**

A frequently asked question is "How large should a board be?" When a board is too large it becomes unwieldy. Seven to nine is a good number for a small or intermediate sized organization. Twelve is still workable, but anything beyond that becomes unwieldy. An organization with a diverse and scattered membership might feel compelled to have larger boards to achieve broad representation.

## Drawing up the list of candidates—and checking it twice

Once you have identified how many new directors are needed, what competencies are needed, and what representational gaps need to be filled, you are ready to start drawing up the *long* list of candidates. The Board Service Committee should be in charge of this process. Throw the net out wide. Look for people with a stellar reputation, strong stature and few known negatives. The CEO might have names to suggest, but I caution against constituting a board made up of friends of the CEO.

In the second step, the long list is pared down to the *short* list, consisting of not more than three of the lead candidates who are then vetted thoroughly. The board should keep on record the files of any persons not making the short list in case it is necessary to re-open the selection process and/or for future openings.

The thoroughness of the vetting process depends on how well the candidates are known. A bad choice can cause havoc with board dynamics and raise questions in the public mind. Unseating a director is more difficult than discharging an unsatisfactory employee. When it is necessary to discharge someone to make room for new blood, do it with the utmost of sensitivity and empathy. Boards should never find themselves so desperate to fill a vacancy that they elect someone with whom they are not well acquainted.

Even candidates who are thought to be well-known may have some dark spots in their pasts. It is good to do some discreet personal checking. At a minimum, you will want to do a Google search, examine the police record, and have a personal interview. Persons completely unknown should be screened more thoroughly, including, without fail, a personal interview.

> **Unseating a director is more difficult than discharging an unsatisfactory employee.**

## Making the ask

Once the board has made its selection, its next challenge is to proposition the candidate in such a way as to increase the likelihood of an affirmative response. It is all an academic exercise until the candidate has confirmed acceptance. I find that when the *right person* is asked at the *right time* and in the *right way*, the likelihood of an acceptance is substantially increased.

Timing of your ask is important. Do not ask someone who is about to have surgery or who has just had a major job change. Do not ask a

**Timing your ask can make all the difference.**

CPA to become your treasurer when they are in the throes of the tax season. Timing your ask can make all the difference.

Consider carefully *how* you ask. Do not be overly casual. Give it the air of importance it deserves. Always do it in person, not by telephone, and never by e-mail. In some cases, do it over a meal or at least a cup of coffee. Many deals are consummated on the golf course. Do whatever works for you, but set the stage for an affirmative reply.

Finally, consider *who* does the asking. I attended a meeting recently when one member volunteered, "Permit me—he owes me big time!" He was deputized

**Big people respond to big challenges. Small bait only attracts small fish.**

and got his trophy! Quid pro quo often works. If you have a really important candidate in mind, get your chairperson to do the asking. It communicates the importance you want to convey.

Whatever you do, do not dumb down the position, hoping to improve your chances of getting an acceptance. That only sets the stage for a lukewarm director. Big people respond to big challenges. Small bait only attracts small fish.

After meeting with a candidate, follow up your ask with a letter summarizing your invitation. Do it before he or she has had an opportunity to reply. Keep the momentum moving in your favor.

## Seating the new director

When the election has occurred, you have one more challenge. That is to help your new member to become a *contributing* member of the board. A thorough orientation can be seen as an acceleration lane. The board chairperson and the CEO should meet with the newly elected member to learn her/his particular interests and abilities. They should provide a packet of materials, including recent board meeting minutes, a copy of the bylaws, and a board manual. The new director should be briefed on the organization's history and current issues. A time of transition is a good time to effect change in your corporate culture and way of doing business.

Your board is now fully constituted, and you are ready to go to work. But before a board can be effective, it must understand its governance role as distinct from the role of management. That is the subject of Chapter 2.

Use the Board Self-Assessment Form included as Exhibit A. Tailor it to your particular circumstances if you wish.

> **A board must understand its governance role as distinct from management.**

## DISCUSSION QUESTIONS

1. Does your board have within its membership the needed competencies?
2. Is your board representative of the membership/supporting body?
3. Does your board have a succession plan to keep it strong and to avoid costly gaps in membership?

**CHAPTER 2**

# Helping Directors Understand Their Governance Role

A n organization is made up of two parts: governance, which is the
responsibility of the board of directors, and management, or operations, which is delegated to the management under the direction of
the CEO. To be effective and to discharge its responsibilities faithfully,
a board must understand this distinction. It is illustrated on page 7.

## The Big X

This appears simple and straightforward, but in experience this
important distinction between governance and management often
becomes unclear, resulting in confusion. When a board understands
this distinction and adheres to it consistently, it becomes easier for
management below the Big X line to define itself. The importance of
this distinction cannot be over emphasized. It is step number one in
organizational effectiveness.

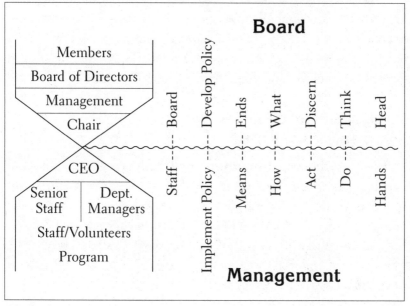

*The Big X*

Governance and management are both necessary, to be sure. They complement each other. They are partners. The German proverb says it well: "One hand washes the other." The line that separates these two organizational functions should, however, not be thought of as a stone wall. The wavy line in the illustration above and the ones that follow is meant to illustrate that the line is negotiable. More on this later.

The distinction I'm making does not preclude directors from engaging in a below-the-Big-X-line activity. A director may flip hamburgers at the annual fundraiser, but when doing so, s/he is serving as a volunteer, perhaps under the direction of a staff member. In this capacity, the director has no board authority. In fact, a director's authority applies only when the board is in session, having a meeting.

> **Governance and management are both necessary, to be sure. They complement each other.**

The responsibility for making this distinction rests first with the board. When the board upholds this distinction, it is easy for management to define itself correctly. When a board abdicates its governance role, or when it becomes excessively involved in management, the result is wholesale confusion and duplication of effort.

## Dividing the function between board and management

Having established the distinction between governance and management, we now address in more detail where this line is drawn in practice. In other words, how is it decided what gets put on the board agenda and what the CEO is authorized/expected to decide on his/her own authority? The two extremes are illustrated below: the Management-Centric X and the Board-Centric X. Then I propose a more ideal approach: the Partnership Model X..

**When I was chairman of Habitat for Humanity International, I participated in four Jimmy Carter blitz builds. I took orders from the house foreperson— whoever that was. I was a volunteer builder like all the others. That I was chairman of the board gave me no special status. A build was not a board event.**

### Management-Centric X

The board's role is minimal. Management has assumed most functions, whether by delegation or default. The board essentially rubber-stamps reports, budgets, and plans prepared by management. The board's role is basically advisory.

Management has taken ownership of the enterprise. It keeps the board generally informed, and the board dutifully approves legal documents that require board action. Beyond that, the board's role is minimal.

### Board-Centric X

Here the board is dominant. It reserves to itself all major decisions, sometimes dipping into management's domain. It prides itself on being hands-on. Its meetings are long and frequent. Its critics say it micro-manages.

Management does as it's told. It is not expected to play a major role in decision-making. In fact, things go better when it doesn't.

### Partnership Model X

The board exercises its fiduciary role through establishing the organization's vision and mission. It delegates implementation to management under the direction of the CEO, along with basic policies that define the sphere within which management is authorized to operate. The board evaluates the performance of the CEO and participates with staff in evaluating program performance annually.

Management accepts its accountability to the board. It assumes responsibility for program implementation within the parameters established by the board. The CEO keeps the board well informed. When a major decision is needed, the CEO brings a recommendation for board approval.

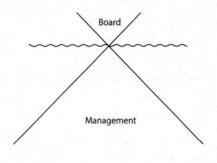

*Management-Centric X*

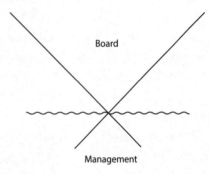

*Board-Centric X*

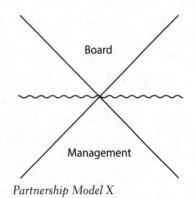

*Partnership Model X*

Some decisions are clearly the responsibility of the board. Others obviously belong to management. But in practice, most decisions fall somewhere in the middle. If the CEO brings too much trivia to the board, the board is kept super busy with mostly the wrong stuff. If s/he usurps too much authority and acts too independently, directors are overheard to grouse, "I'm not sure what we are here for—management decides everything any way." It is at this point of ambiguity that many misunderstandings occur.

Where this line is drawn varies and is, in any case, arbitrary. The board of a young/small organization is of necessity more board-centric than a large organization with a large professional staff. When a board is inexperienced and the CEO is an old veteran, the line is drawn at a different place than if the inverse is true. The important thing is that both sides respect the line wherever it is drawn and that there be consistency in the tasks expected of the board and of the staff.

This line also needs to be adjusted as an organization matures. When an organization is young and/or small, the directors are hardly aware of the division of function. Directors do both until they drop over from exhaustion. As the organization grows, the board agenda gets longer, and higher standards of performance are expected. Directors get fatigued, so more functions are delegated to management. It is called growing up.

In the past two decades, the tendency has been for nonprofit boards to follow the lead of for profit boards and to become more CEO-centric. More time is needed to determine if this trend is good or bad.

It pains me to admit that occasionally an unprincipled CEO may pretend to be engaging the board with meaningless trivia, while, in fact, s/he is doing an end run around the board. It is not the formula for a long and trusting relationship. A board must keep that from happening, without, however, moving to the other extreme.

Few boards, in my experience, draw this distinguishing line between board work and staff by deliberate action. Mostly it happens by default and somewhat arbitrarily, on a case by case basis, until a pattern emerges.

The interplay between the chair and the CEO compares to a dance complete with the occasional stumbles. The relationship between these two officeholders is without equal. If they get it right, the incidence of misdirected energy is materially reduced within the entire organization, and the stage is set for effective governance.

Having now seated a competent board and defined its role in relationship to the operations, we are now ready to discuss in more detail the six duties of a board.

## DISCUSSION QUESTIONS

1. Does your board understand and practice its governance function as distinct from management, as illustrated in the Big X?
2. Does your board need to review and update the division of function between the board and management (CEO) as illustrated with the three Xs?
3. Are the board and management (CEO) functioning as an effective partnership? Do they understand and respect their own individual roles and the role of the other?

# CHAPTER 3

# Defining the Purpose— Duty #1

O rganizations exist for a purpose. An organization without a purpose is like a car without wheels. The first duty of a board is to define that purpose and state it in clear and compelling terms. A statement of purpose lays out what the board, in its fiduciary capacity, is undertaking to accomplish on behalf of its members or constituents. Directors begin this process by addressing three basic questions:

1. **What do our members or constituents expect?** Why do they support the effort? Although these expectations are seldom stated in written form, members and constituents have them, and they are entitled to them.

   Directors must be alert to these expectations. Good directors have good antennas. They have their ears to the ground. They take careful note of what members do or do not

**Good directors have good antennas.**

support, what they value, what they will not tolerate, and whom they elect.

Expectations will change over time, and there are occasions when directors must educate members. But in the end, an organization is viable only if its activities are understood and supported by its constituency.

2. **What need are we addressing?** This line of inquiry will help to answer Peter Drucker's rhetorical question: "What is our business?" A board answers this question in its vision and mission statements that guide program formulation. A successful organization always has a defined purpose, even as an airplane pilot always has a destination.

There are well over a million nonprofit organizations in the United States and Canada, all focused on defined needs. They may be as varied as schools, hospitals, or a Society for the Preservation of Covered Bridges. Directors must identify the particular need to which they feel called, which must be consistent with member expectations.

3. **What are our resources?** What do we have or what can we get by way of staff, money, or materials with which to address this need meaningfully?

What do we know, and what are we competent to do? Organizations must resist the temptation to be all things to all people; to chase popular causes; to overestimate themselves and underestimate what is needed.

> **Organizations must resist the temptation to be all things to all people.**

Nothing is served by do-gooders undertaking activities that are outside of their competence or resources.

Having answered these foundational questions, a board addresses in greater depth and detail the issues of vision, mission, and values.

**Vision** states the purpose for which an organization exists and, maybe more importantly, what it wants to *become*. Vision imagines something that is not yet but could or should be. Vision drives out the status quo. It liberates organizations from old routines and gives them a reason to exist. In the words of Robert Browning, "Ah, but a man's reach should exceed his grasp, or what's a heaven for?"

Vision statements are strategic. They look past the daily routine and identify something to grow into.

In defining its vision, an organization sets aside everyday limitations and frustrations to imagine what it wants most to become. The best vision statements are bold and concise. Once a vision statement is adopted, it becomes the standard against which actions are measured.

> **The best vision statements are bold and concise.**

In a visioning exercise, you are freed from the ubiquitous question, "Can we afford it?" to ask instead, "What would we like to do or become that is beyond our reach now?" Then bend every effort to make it happen. People are doing it everyday. That is how the world of organizations turns.

Sometimes I think the best philosophy appears on the sports page. An NFL football phenom who won games with Hail Mary passes was quoted as saying, "If you believe, unbelievable things can happen."

Average boards orient themselves around the rearview mirror—precedent is their big thing. They examine everything under the microscope; they want to avoid mistakes. Great boards look through a telescope to planets beyond—at what could be—and ask, "Why not?"

**Mission** is what an organization commits itself to *do*. It identifies a clear, compelling, and achievable goal. Whereas vision is a dream, a stretch, mission is a commitment: "This we will do." Whereas vision

> **Vision reaches for the stars; *mission* is grounded in the here and now.**

reaches for the stars, mission is grounded in the here and now. Organizations need both—vision to identify the more distant goal, and mission to zero in on the means by which the identified vision is realized.

**A mental health facility had a successful inpatient treatment program. When the need shifted to outpatient treatment, it transitioned to satellite clinics. It adjusted its program to respond to market realities. It prospered, while those who stayed with the old model found themselves on the margins.**

Organizations tend to get locked into what they know and are already doing. The challenging reality of our world is that about the time we get comfortable with what we are doing, it is moving toward extinction. To survive, organizational leaders need to be nimble and yet grounded. When an organization stays with the old too long, it is forced to make radical changes. Great organizations change with the changing times. Those who refuse to change disappear. It is that simple.

A vision statement identifies the strategic goal to which you aspire. The mission is fulfilled by the annual work plan. These two foundational statements are drawn up by the board with strong participation by management.

**Values** inform *how* the goal is achieved. Great organizations are not only concerned about getting things done; they want things done in ways that are consistent with their stated values.

A clear and compelling sense of purpose gives an organization energy to do great things. If a journey begins with a destination, an organization begins by knowing for what purpose it exists.

# DISCUSSION QUESTIONS

1. Is your board clear on the purpose for which it exists? Is that purpose expressed clearly and concisely in the following ways?
   a) Statement of vision—what you want to become.
   b) Statement of mission—what you commit yourself to accomplish.
   c) Statement of values—the values you are committed to work by.
2. Are these statements consulted when the board deliberates? Do they influence decision-making?
3. Are these statements reviewed periodically and revised as circumstances suggest?

# CHAPTER 4

# Planning to Fulfill the Purpose—Duty #2

After a board has clarified the purpose for which it exists, it must devise a plan to achieve it. Vision and mission statements are only fine-sounding phrases until they begin to operate.

Planning is the link between what is and what is to be. It is the gateway to the future. Planning is not an event. It is an ongoing process that identifies what is working well and builds on that, while weeding out what is no longer contributing to the identified mission.

> **Planning is the link between what is and what is to be.**

Planning should be part of every board's routine. Great boards periodically set aside routine business, which often presents itself with undeserved urgency, to concentrate on formulating a plan by which its identified purpose will be realized. This requires determination and discipline. It is a necessary step on the pathway to greatness. Organizations exist to do, and for that they need to plan.

This chapter, as much of the book, assumes a medium-sized organization. Both plans need to be tailored to the size, age and unique circumstances of a particular organization.

## Long-range plan

Organizations need both a strategic long-range plan and an annual work plan. The two are related but distinct. The long-range plan reaches beyond what is possible today and aspires to what is so far only imagined. This plan identifies a need before the capacity is there to address it. It entertains what is now beyond its reach and makes every effort to realize it. Planning can be thought of as walking a dream into existence.

**Planning can be thought of as walking a dream into existence.**

Visionary planning drives out the status quo. It has passion that liberates an organization from drowsy routines and gives it a reason to exist. Vision is focused on the future.

Most organizations live too much in the present and the past. "The board's domain," I am fond of saying, "is the future." If by some stroke of good fortune, organizations were to receive a million dollars, most of them wouldn't know what to do with it. They think and plan in small increments. They have no vision beyond the immediate. Their planning horizon is too short. Your reach should exceed your grasp.

## Annual plan

Whereas a long-range plan is vision, the annual work plan is a commitment. "This we will do; count on it." The annual plan is drawn from the long-range plan and is the process by which it is fulfilled.

**A long-range plan is vision; the annual work plan is a commitment.**

It is not enough to be busy. Everyone is busy. And the annual work plan is more than good intentions. Organizations need to be specific about what they are committed to *accomplish.* The annual work plan establishes specific goals and activities by which the vision will be realized. It states what will be done (outcomes), who will do it, where, how, by when, and with what. Its progress can be monitored and measured.

## Who plans?

The short answer is that everyone plans on his or her level. As planning moves up the organizational hierarchy, the planning horizons get longer. John Carver, the policy governance guru, likes to use the metaphor of stacking mixing bowls. The board is the big bowl. Its planning is all-encompassing. The next, and slightly smaller, bowl represents senior management, and so on, until everyone is accounted for, including the ground crew.

**Everyone plans on his or her level.**

Planning at the board level should invite the full participation of management. In that sense, it straddles the previously mentioned Big X line. The simple fact is that many issues come to a board from management, so management should have a place at the planning table. In the end, however, the final decision for the macro-plan rests with the board.

## Planning input

Whereas visioning has in it elements of dreaming and imagining, annual planning begins in the here and now and builds toward that identified future. A planning exercise begins by doing the following:

1. Complete a thorough examination of your vision and mission statements. Do they state in clear and compelling words what you aspire to become (vision) and what you are committed to do to get there (mission)? Perhaps these statements need to be tweaked or rewritten. They are the North Star to guide your planning and decision-making.

2. Survey the universe in which you live, and ask yourself what is needed. Needs are constantly changing. Don't be like the Swiss watch industry that kept making quality spring watches while the world was going digital. Be early to recognize change on the horizon and adjust accordingly.

3. Review the evaluation of your present program (see Chapter 7). What is soaring and should be expanded? What is winding down and should be phased out? What appears to be waiting for its turn under the sun and should be introduced?

   Great organizations are guided by need. They do not resist change. They seek to understand it and then build their program in response to it. Sometimes it is necessary to trim back or even chop down the old trees in order to get sunlight to the young trees.

4. Always be mindful of your constituents. What do they want? What do they value? What will they support?

5. Finally, assess what you know. What are you qualified to do by way of staff or resources, available or obtainable?

**Great organizations are guided by need.**

## Participatory planning

Since the nonprofit board is responsible to deliver on constituent expectations, it begins the process of macro-planning by establishing the broad perimeters by which management will put the plan into operation. The focus of the board in this stage is on *what* should be done, leaving the *how* it should be done for management to determine. Board planning is therefore done in close collaboration with senior management by answering the following questions:

1. What current activities should be increased?
2. What activities should be reduced or terminated?
3. What new activities should be introduced?

Next, the board establishes how much money will be available for program. This step results in just one number, but one of gigantic importance. If the board is too ambitious, the result will be frustration and disappointment. If it is too cautious, the organization will underperform what is possible. In an ongoing organization, this number is often expressed in a percent of the current budget, either up or down.

Within these perimeters the board authorizes management, under the direction of the CEO, to draw up the annual work plan, complete with a line item budget. The board states when the recommended plan should be available for review and gives instructions pertaining to the reporting format.

I prefer a presentation that begins with an executive summary of not too many pages (depending on the size of the organization) with the details in attachments as needed. The plan should be sufficiently specific to permit evaluation.

Management then recommends its plan to the board for approval. The board should receive it appreciatively but not superficially. The plan proposes where the organization's resources will be focused in the next year. The board has the right to amend the plan management brings.

Both the board and management own the final approved plan. Both participated in drafting it. Both are totally committed to its fulfillment.

## Planning is dynamic

President Eisenhower was fond of saying, "I learned long ago that plans are worthless; planning is everything." Planning is dynamic because it takes changing circumstances into account. A five-year plan, for example, is not expected to last five years. It should be reviewed annually and changed as suggested by experience. An

> **An organization should always be in the first year of a multi-year plan.**

organization, it is said, should always be in the first year of a multi-year plan.

Tom Peters warns in a similar vein against holding plans too tightly. Plans are servant, not master. Plans belong to us, not we to them. Plans can and should be changed as the circumstances to which they apply change. But activity should always be guided by a plan, within the context of a macro-plan.

"Organizations that fail to plan," said one organizational expert, "plan to fail."

## DISCUSSION QUESTIONS

1. Does your board have a long-range plan to realize the more distant vision it has of itself? For example, "By the year _____, we will _____."
2. Does your board have an annual work plan and budget, complete with goals that can be evaluated to eventually realize the stated vision?
3. Is your board planning in sync with management? Has management participated in drawing up these plans? Is it committed to their fulfillment?

# CHAPTER 5

# Fulfilling the Purpose Through Delegation— Duty #3

The effectiveness of any plan is only as good as its implementation. Directors do very little of the doing. They decide what should be done and then *delegate* implementation to management under the direction of the CEO, or, in a small/young organization, to a special committee. Effective delegation together with appropriate supervision is, therefore, the process by which a board's decisions are translated into results.

## The role of the CEO

All program administration in medium or large organizations emanates from and/or passes through the office of the CEO. This helps to explain why it is sometimes said that

> **The effectiveness of any decision is only as good as its implementation.**

**The value of an executive is in how he or she is able to enlist and motivate others.**

the appointment of the CEO and the subsequent relationship to the rest of the staff is second to none.

The CEO is the only person who is responsible directly to the board. All other staff and volunteers report to the CEO. The value of an executive is not in how hard s/he works, but in how well he or she is able to direct and motivate others.

Even as a good CEO cares for those under his or her direction, so a great board cares for its CEO. In doing so, it sets a good example for the entire organization. An enduring relationship begins with a thorough, well-thought-out job description. A job description should state what the CEO is responsible to *accomplish*. It is focused on expected outcomes, not activities.

(The annual review of the board/CEO relationship is discussed in more detail in Chapter 7 and Exhibit B.)

## Delegation with policy guidance

CEOs have broad authority, but they are not free to do as they think best on all matters. A good board establishes the parameters within which the CEO uses discretion.

John Carver, an authority on organizational governance, says simply, "All board activity should be governed by policy." Some boards have adopted the Carver model of policy governance and report good results, while others find it excessively complex. My observation is that it works best in large organizations with highly professional directors.

As an organization grows and matures, the board meets its responsibility by adopting a set of policies to guide implementation of the approved program. Policies should be seen as instruction for now and the future, based on experience. Some say, mistakenly, that this puts the CEO in a box. To the contrary, policies help the CEO know what is expected and what will not be tolerated.

The secret is in finding the right middle ground for your organization. When a board surrounds its CEO with too many policies, the CEO does not have the freedom needed to be effective, and the board is overburdened. A strong CEO will not put up with it. It is demeaning.

Complex issues do not lend themselves to prescribed policies; they require individual attention. How capable a board is in dealing with such issues is a measure of its effectiveness. They are one reason why a board is needed.

When the board is not sufficiently defined through the policies it has adopted, both the CEO and the board operate in an atmosphere of uncertainty.

## Organizational maturation

One of the stiffest challenges organizations face is adjusting their governance to respond to growth and changes in the environment. Successfully navigating through this era can lead to bigger and better things.

A music station I enjoy listening to uses the phrase "Everything was once new." And so it was, and so organizations we serve were once new. Organizations begin small, and as they grow, changes need to be made in their management. Failure to do so results in organizational stunting, which is more common than most of us would like to admit.

Small can be beautiful, and big is not always better. Participating in an organization that is in its infancy can be an exhilarating experience. So let there be no feelings of inferiority about smallness or youthfulness.

Size is, nevertheless, an important consideration in how a board defines its governance work. *Small/young organizations need to be managed and cared for differently from big organizations.* This pertains especially to planning and delegation.

In an organization's youth, the Big X is less applicable, although even at that stage there is value in distinguishing *what* (shall be done) from *how*. They are two halves that make a whole.

Most nonprofit organizations are birthed in a euphoric atmosphere. This idea will "Save the world." They decide what should be done, and then they go about doing it with gusto. They may even be living out the German proverb, "Everybody is doing what they want to do. Nobody is doing what they should be doing. But everyone is enthusiastically engaged."

Eventually the newness wears off, the founders get tired, and it becomes clear that amateurish volunteerism does not cut it any more. So the leaders organize committees. Then more committees. What else, who else, is there?

When things wear thin again, someone in a low moment may venture to say, "Maybe a CEO wouldn't be such a bad idea after all." At Habitat affiliates, making the jump to employing a CEO became a kind of rite of passage to bigger and better things. (Even amid frustrations and disappointments, some devoted pioneers later refer nostalgically to these pre-CEO times as the "good old days.")

> **Making the jump to employing a CEO can become a rite of passage to bigger and better things.**

As organizations grow, more functions are transferred from the board (above the line) to management (below the line.) Now the Big X line diagram begins to appear. The board function becomes more supervisory. This can be a challenging time in the life of an organization because it requires a different kind of leadership. Sometime this transition can be aided through director education; sometimes it requires new blood.

Introducing a CEO into what has been a volunteer driven organization is not as simple as it appears. Volunteer directors must step back from roles to which they have become attached to make room for the CEO. This is not always easy and can result in frustration and duplication of effort. Sadly, the first CEO is too often a casualty.

## Delegation is a two-step process

The first step in delegating is authorizing the CEO to proceed with staff to implement the approved plan, along with whatever instructions (policies) are appropriate and needed. Then the board steps back while the management does its work. The board does not interfere or disappear. It observes.

The second step is supervision. A board has a need and a right to know if the plans were implemented that they had approved. If so, did they produce the desired results? Outcomes are always in the backs of directors' minds as they monitor progress.

Along the way, many ventures may appear doomed. Many projects, it is true, pass through a valley of disappointment before they bear fruit. Deciding if a project that is off to a slow start will right itself over time, or if it is a boondoggle and needs to discontinue, is one of the hardest decisions boards and executives are called on to make.

In all of this, but especially in delegating, the board works in close partnership with management. Each knows its role and respects the role of the other. All are dedicated to deliver on the "contract" they have with their members or constituents.

## DISCUSSION QUESTIONS

1. Has your board delegated plan implementation to management with instructions (policies) that embody the organization's stated values? Does management know its prerogatives and responsibilities with regard to plan implementation?

2. Does your board have enough policies? Or too many? Are the policies readily available in a policy manual with a user-friendly table of contents?
3. Does your board have reporting procedures in place that permit it to appropriately monitor what is or is not happening?
4. Does the board perform its supervisory function without meddling in the role of management?

# CHAPTER 6

# Resourcing the Plan— Duty #4

Plan implementation requires resources. In everyday language, that equates to money and staff.

"Money," said one of the best treasurers I've been privileged to know, "isn't everything, but it sure beats whatever is in second place." That was spoken as a typical treasurer but not without a point. Money is important, but an organization's resources go beyond money and include both assets that are recorded in a ledger as well as non-ledger assets.

> **An organization's resources go beyond money.**

## Ledger assets

Ledger assets consist of money and physical property. Many nonprofit organizations scrimp along on very little money while others have assets that range into the billions. In 2010 there were 1.4 million 501(c)(3) organizations in the United States, with income totaling $286 billion. They had 13.7 million employees (10% of the U.S. labor force), plus no one knows how many hours of contributed volunteer labor. Not bad for a sector that is known for what it is not—profit! Additionally, there is the substantial activity of more than 300,000 churches and the large mutual insurance sector.

A budget is a very necessary and useful administrative tool in managing an organization's resources. Budgeting allows us to anticipate if projected income will be adequate to finance our approved plan. Any imbalance must be corrected by either increasing income or decreasing expenses, to say the obvious.

The work of fundraising and accounting may be delegated to staff or a committee of the board, but the board remains responsible to ensure that the funds are available to fulfill the approved plan. To approve a plan or budget without the requisite resources in hand—or without a realistic plan to raise them—is irresponsible.

Day to day money management functions are delegated to management, but boards are expected to exercise prudent *oversight* of all financial activity. Boards commonly do this through the following practices:

> **Boards are expected to exercise prudent oversight over all of an organization's financial activity.**

1. Approval of an annual budget that distributes funds in accordance with plans approved by the board, with appropriate financial reporting throughout the year;
2. An annual independent financial audit with follow-up as necessary;
3. Risk management, including the purchase of insurance;
4. Prudent cash flow management procedures requiring that all income be deposited and all disbursements be made by check, requiring dual check signing authority.

Some organizations have substantial investment accounts that need to be well managed.

Persons who are authorized to invest those funds do well to heed the advice of Warren Buffett, the billionaire investment guru, whose first rule of investing is not to lose money. The second rule is not to forget the first rule.

## Non-ledger assets

**The ability to attract and retain strong staff separates the good from the great.**

Assets that cannot be recorded in a ledger are less visible, but they may be even more valuable than hard assets. I think of them in two categories:

1. **Personnel.** The old dictum says it well, "You are only as good as your help." The ability to attract and retain strong staff separates the good from the great. Much of this responsibility resides below the line with management, but there is also a board dimension. The board can discharge its responsibility through mandating the following practices:

- Job descriptions for all positions, written with outcomes in mind—and not merely activities. What do we expect?
- An organizational chart to describe relationships. Who is responsible to whom?
- An annual performance appraisal procedure beginning with the CEO but used throughout the whole organization. I am attracted to a recent practice of supplementing the monitoring of job descriptions with a coaching approach to increase performance. How well are we doing?
- A salary and benefit scale, including a personal growth plan for all employees. How much pay and benefits do staff receive?
- A grievance procedure to be followed when things go wrong—as they will, even in the best organizations. How do we deal with adversity?

- Exit interviews for outgoing employees. If good staff is leaving your organization voluntarily, a good board (and management) wants to know why. The board, or a committee of the board, may not read each exit interview report, but the board should require that such a procedure be in place.

Great boards know the importance of good staff. They look for ways to affirm this valuable asset and, together with the CEO, create a pleasant and stimulating work environment.

2. **Image/Reputation.** "A good name is better than great riches," said Solomon, thought to have been the wisest man ever. It is also apropos for nonprofits that depend on public support. Indeed, reputation is more valuable than an American Express card. Reputation is earned over decades, but it can be lost in one ill-advised act.

> **Reputation is earned over many years and can be lost in one careless act.**

It is no longer good enough for nonprofits to go quietly about doing a good job. Healthy charities look for appropriate ways to promote and safeguard their brand. Build your image. Protect your image. Promote your image. It is a public charity's most valuable asset.

Survival and delivery of services are an organization's ultimate tests. To serve, organizations must survive. To survive, organizations must serve. Survival does not mean just getting by. To be healthy, organizations need to thrive. They need to build a can-do reputation. The public wants and deserves bang for the buck. Obsolescence, sloth, and apathy must be avoided like the plague.

What is the worth of morale? Of teamwork? Of loyalty? Of trust? Of goodwill? It all starts in the boardroom. Adopting a grandiose plan without providing the enabling resources serves no purpose. A plan is good only if it is accompanied by the resources needed for its fulfillment. This is another area for board and management collaboration, but ultimately the responsibility resides with the board.

> **A plan is good only if it is accompanied by the resources needed for its fulfillment.**

## DISCUSSION QUESTIONS

1. Does your board have in place a system that will ensure that the resources needed to fulfill the plan are available? (See Chapter 15: The Board Role in Fundraising, page 75.)
2. Is your board demonstrating good stewardship of its ledger and non-ledger resources?
3. Do you protect and promote your brand sufficiently?

# CHAPTER 7

# Monitoring and Evaluating Performance—Duty #5

E very organization that receives its support from the public, whether large or small, religious or secular, young or old, has an obligation to evaluate its performance. It is not enough for directors to plan and delegate and then disappear. Remembering their fiduciary roles (to act on behalf of), great directors are continually asking themselves if they are delivering on their "contract" with their members?

Monitoring and evaluating performance are among the most commonly neglected board duties. They are also two of the most basic duties of a board.

## Why do many boards neglect evaluation?

1. They are complacent and skeptical of its usefulness. "Why should we?" "What would it accomplish?" "Things are going just fine." "If it ain't broke, don't fix it."

2. They don't know how. "How do we put an objective value on what is basically a subjective activity?" "We might end up doing more harm than good." "Let good enough alone."
3. They are pressed for time. "I have no objection, but where are you going to find time for such an academic exercise?" "You see how full our agendas are." It's just not a priority.

So how do we assign objective value to an activity that is so subjective? Some things can be quantified, but not all. Jim Collins, in *Good to Great*, says, "To throw up our hands and say, 'But we cannot measure performance in the social sectors the way you can in business' is simply a lack of discipline." Minimally, we can establish a baseline and measure ourselves against our organization's own previous performance.

Others ask, "Won't a bad evaluation be discouraging?" To the contrary, when you fail to measure, you have no way to track progress, and that is the precursor to discouragement.

## Great boards evaluate themselves

Of three areas boards should be evaluating, I suggest beginning with the one that is most important and the one boards are least likely to undertake: evaluating themselves, their own performance as a board. Lethargy in the boardroom spreads like a virus. When the board is asleep at the wheel, soon the whole organization is drowsy if not in a deep sleep. Remember, organizations, like trees, die from the top.

**Lethargy in the boardroom spreads like a virus.**

Boards are urged to reserve an entire meeting for looking back (evaluating) and looking ahead (dreaming and planning). It could be the most important meeting of the year. Some prefer to do it in a retreat-type setting.

To help your board evaluate its performance, consider using Exhibit A on page 125. Adapt it for your use. Try, as much as possible, to use basically the same form year after year so you can compare performances.

I strongly recommend inviting the CEO, and perhaps members of the senior staff, to participate. It will give another dimension and foster a spirit of teamwork.

Sometimes you may want to invite an outside facilitator, but I urge you not to turn this important function over entirely to an outsider. This should be an occasion when you draw on your own inner resources and address the issues you know better than anyone else.

The evaluation agenda should zero in on subjects closely related to your key functions. But be sure to reserve some quality time to anticipate the future. Plan, too, to interact with each other and learn to know each other better. Have some fun.

Having set an example for the entire organization by evaluating your own performance as a governing board, you are ready now to address the other two things great boards evaluate.

## Great boards evaluate the performance of their CEO

If the appointment of a CEO is a board's single most important decision, it follows that fostering this relationship is of utmost importance. It begins with a good job description that must establish three things:

1. To whom is the CEO responsible? CEOs are usually thought to be responsible to the board via the chair.
2. Who is responsible to the CEO? The stock answer is, "All employees and volunteers, directly or indirectly." (This is a good time to ask for an organogram or organizational chart.)
3. What is the CEO responsible for? The stock answer is, "All operations." The emphasis should be on outcomes (results to be achieved), not activities.

In my experience, this is not always as straightforward as it appears. Boards tend to make exceptions, sometimes resulting in great confusion. Boards monitor what is going on below the Big X line, and in the process they sometimes overstep. One particular fault line is where board committees interact with senior staff, sometimes bypassing the CEO or even the board. The annual evaluation is a good time to sort out these working relationships before they become conflicted.

Only after you have clarified what the CEO is responsible for are you ready to evaluate if and to what extent he or she is doing what the board expects.

The review itself should be a two-way conversation. It is not only the CEO's performance that is being reviewed. It is the all-important *relationship* between the board and the CEO, too. Sometimes board members are creating

> **The review should be a two-way conversation.**

problems they are unaware of. Sometimes a board expects things the CEO has not understood.

Be clear. In the end you want the CEO to be energized and affirmed, not beaten down.

An outline for the annual review is found in Exhibit B (page 130).

## Great boards evaluate operations

When monitoring what is happening below the Big X line a board must collaborate with the CEO. This is where the board's fiduciary role is especially pertinent. Directors are asking on behalf of the members and constituents questions like the following:

1. Do our program activities align well with our stated mission and values? Are we doing the right things? In the right way?
2. To what extent are our board-approved goals and objectives being realized? What are our outcomes? Are people's lives being changed? Does our organization make a difference?

3. Are our activities cost-effective? Are they an efficient use of money and personnel?
4. Where are our programs on their life cycles? What is winding down? What is emerging to replace it?
5. Are we well positioned for the future? What changes do we observe in the environment? In resources available with which to fuel programs?
6. How effective is our delivery system?

**The jump from good to great is based on honest evaluation.**

To borrow a term from stonemasons, "Work your mud." Strive for improvement. Be reminded, "Everything can be improved," as the foreign car company ad says. The jump from good to great is based on honest evaluation.

Do not, I repeat, do *not* consider your work completed until your evaluation has been condensed into written resolutions that can be tracked. What appears to be eminently clear now will be blurry when you want to consult the results of this evaluation to influence next year's program planning. Retain in written form changes you want to see in the future. Assign someone who is capable to produce this document.

## Outside evaluation

While a board's main source of program evaluation comes from management, it should not be the only source. It is simply human nature to overreport success and to turn a blind eye to failure, or even to hide it. Beyond a certain point, those closest to the program lose their objectivity. The for-profit world is much better at cutting its losses and running than the nonprofit sector is. Major programs should open themselves to being reviewed periodically by knowledgeable persons from a variety of backgrounds.

I was directing the Mennonite Central Committee program when we were making a major transition from relief to development. At the staff level we were like a boy with a new toy. The Executive Committee, informed by our own staff reports, observed that in our enthusiasm we were neglecting those programs where relief was the better response. When we were resistant to their counsel, they took us to the woodshed, and appropriately so. Sometimes staff, with all its closeness, loses objectivity, while a somewhat more removed body has a more objective view.

## Getting started

The hardest part of evaluating is breaking into our oppressive routine and reserving the time to get started. Evaluation requires commitment and some new thinking, but it is worth it. Performance almost always improves, which in turn increases the satisfaction of board and staff alike. Before long you will say, "We should have done this sooner."

# DISCUSSION QUESTIONS

1. Does your board reserve some time every year to take a hard, objective look at itself and how it does its work? Do you occasionally have board training sessions?

2. Does your board perform an annual review with its CEO to clarify mutual expectations and agreed-on priorities? (See also Exhibit B: CEO Annual Review Outline, page 130).

3. Does your board, with management, evaluate program performance annually to confirm that goals are being met and to identify needed changes? Are member expectations being met?

CHAPTER 8

# Serving the Membership— Duty #6

**D**irectors do not own the enterprise. Members or constituents do. The board is obligated to keep them well informed. Doing so is also in the board's best interests. A loyal and supportive constituency is more valuable than money in the bank. Bank balances get depleted, but a loyal, well-informed constituency is a renewable resource. It is a wellspring.

## Know the membership

To serve your members or constituents well, you need to know them. Community-based organizations are surrounded by their constituencies. They know their members and what they expect and value. This makes it possible for boards to report to them and thank them in person.

National or even international organizations, by way of contrast, need to look for other ways to interact with their memberships. Regardless of how it is done, an organization that receives its support from the public must continually make efforts to stay in meaningful contact with its members.

When I served on the Habitat board, we engaged a consultant to perform a profile of our widely scattered support base. We were amazed by what we learned. We had assumed that our biggest donors were men with deep pockets, and had directed our publicity accordingly. We were surprised to discover that our support base was primarily older women whose average donations were less than $100. Knowing this permitted us to beam our publicity more accurately, with improved results.

## Serving the membership

The unfortunate fact is that the only time many organizations address their members is when they are asking them for money. This caused one person to observe with scathing accuracy, "Sheep need to be fed daily and can be sheared only once a year!" To this I add, from personal experience, "And when sheep are sheared too often, their skins get sore."

> **Unfortunately, the only time many organizations address their members is when they are asking them for money.**

Constituents want, above all, to know—and they have a right to know—if the objectives of the organization are being achieved. Are lives being changed? Did their contributions make a difference?

Human interest stories count for more than slick brochures. In fact, slick is sometimes a turn-off. Donors look for evidence of outcomes. Much publicity concentrates on inputs—so many dollars, so many workers, and so many tons of this and that—with almost no reference to outcomes. Yet results are what it's all about.

Nonprofits can learn about keeping their base well informed from the for-profit world that addresses its annual reports to the stockholders. Nonprofits might get better results if they addressed their reports to their constituents.

## Honesty in publicity

Many organizations report only the positive things that happen. They hide the shadows and exaggerate the accomplishments. That may work for a time, but it is not the way to build a solid, enduring support base. You can, it is said, tell a big lie with a hundred truths.

Enduring relationships are predicated on openness and honesty. Publicity that hides the difficulties that have been encountered under-estimates the donors' abilities to understand disappointments and unforeseen reversals. It is a mistake and an insult to flood members with success stories that only faintly resemble reality.

When problems are glossed over or ignored—to say nothing of denied—the membership becomes cynical and suspicious. Dishonest or incomplete reporting is like building your fundraising house on sand. It won't last. Sharing a program disappointment can, in fact, be an opportunity to increase respect and trust, and therefore increase donor support.

I crossed an organization off my list, which I had long supported, because I knew from other sources that they were experiencing huge difficulties and disappointments. But they gave no hint of it in their publicity. I concluded, "They are not being honest with me." Some of their difficulties could have been explained, but by denying them they violated my trust.

Transparency and honesty go hand in hand. When I served with the Mennonite Central Committee, which incidentally has a wonder-fully supportive constituency, I was fond of saying, "If I cannot explain something we are doing to the remotest part of our constituency, both geographically and philosophically, we probably should not to be doing it." Your membership needs to know—and understand—what you are doing.

## Fundraising

Fundraising efforts succeed only when they are built on a foundation of trust and proven competence. Constituents are by definition already donors, so we are talking about continuing and increasing their support and enlisting them to attract new donors.

Fundraisers know that current contributors are their best prospects for future giving. How much donors give to any one of the many deserving causes that appeal to them depends on how well they have been sold on the causes presented to them. You want your members to see themselves as enduring partners, not names in some database.

> **Current contributors are the best prospects for future contributions.**

## A role for directors

Directors can add valuable support to fundraising efforts by serving as ambassadors for the cause. They can be the links to the wider constituency. They can and should open doors through their personal and professional networks. They can quash rumors and spread good will.

Every board member should have what is sometimes called an elevator speech that they are prepared to give at a service club or wherever on a moment's notice. It may be only one minute in length, but if it conveys enthusiasm for the cause, it can be invaluable.

## A word of caution

Directors must be careful not to divulge board confidences and publicly launder disputes that may be raging within the board. Being transparent does not extend to divulging board confidences.

A publicly supported organization is healthy and has a secure future only if it has a loyal, well-informed supporting constituency. Money and time invested in servicing the membership is well spent. (More information on fundraising is found in Chapter 15, page 75.)

## Evaluating the six duties

All six duties of a board of directors are necessary and need to be completed with consistency. To evaluate how well your board is performing these duties, I urge you to complete the Board Self-Assessment Form in Exhibit A, on page 125. It will help you to see quickly where improvement is most needed. Some boards do this during a board retreat. Some are even so bold as to invite senior staff to complete the form as well. Their perspectives are sometimes different and yet relevant.

Regardless of how well you are functioning, there is always room for improvement. It is through self-evaluation that good boards become great boards. Improvement at the board level is quickly reflected throughout the whole organization. Soon the entire organization will be *Doing Good Better*!

> **Improvement at the board level is quickly reflected throughout the whole organization.**

## DISCUSSION QUESTIONS

1.  How well does your board know its membership and what they value and expect?
2.  How well does your board keep its membership or constituency informed?
3.  Do a little introspection. How well are your board and the programs understood by your membership or constituency? How can you increase ownership and deepen loyalty?

# CHAPTER 9

# Better Meetings

ave you ever asked yourself, "Why should we have meetings? Some are so contentious and seem so futile!" A cynic was overheard to say, "Meetings are where you keep minutes and lose hours. Couldn't we just do away with them?" Even the Bible weighs in with "Your meetings do more harm than good." (I Corinthians 11:17)

Well, no! The only time that a board functions as a board is when it is in session, having a meeting. The quality of a board's work is therefore judged by the quality of its meetings. The boardroom is the board's workshop.

"But must there be so many meetings? Maybe they could be shorter and more productive." Exactly.

It is really quite simple. Meetings—both board and committee meetings—are expected to accomplish two things. Just two. Everything else is not board business. The two purposes of a meeting are:

1. **Informational:** Boards operate mostly from second-hand information, usually provided by management. This information must be

reliable, accurate, and comprehensive. A board's decisions can only be as good as the information on which they are based.

The same is true for committees. In many organizations, committees take up more time than the board. Committees, it should be clear, do not act for the board. They prepare issues for the board to then act on. Committee work is always subject to board approval.

2. **Decision-making:** A board is judged by the decisions it makes. Some boards do little more than receive and approve reports, with deep appreciation, of course! They make few decisions of any consequence. Either nothing is happening, or the decision-making process is circumventing the board. Both are troublesome signs.

## Conducting effective meetings

Effective board work begins with effective meetings. Many things go into making a meeting effective, not the least of which is a spirit of collaboration within the board and between board and management. Board work is teamwork. It is as much listening as talking. It is discerning. It is asking good questions. President Lyndon Johnson used to quote Isaiah 1:18, "Come now and let us reason together."

Many meetings are, truth be told, a colossal waste of time. Ten directors meeting for four hours constitute one workweek. The results do not always justify the investment of time and effort. My hunch is that many organizations would use board and committee meeting time better if they had to pay for it.

## Meeting agenda

Great meetings begin with a well-planned agenda. Planning for the next meeting should begin immediately after the preceding meeting adjourns. That is the best time to identify the issues that need to be addressed and to make assignments. It

**Planning an effective meeting begins immediately after the preceding meeting adjourns.**

allows the next meeting to build on the previous one and avoids the discontinuity so characteristic of many boards whose directors have other preoccupations.

The chairperson and the CEO draw up the agenda together. If the chairperson is responsible for how the board functions, as we advocate, it follows logically that the chairperson should participate in agenda preparation. It is equally logical that the CEO should participate since he or she is closest to the program, which is where many board issues originate. In practice, the CEO commonly produces the first draft and then asks the chairperson to review it before it is distributed.

The agenda identifies what will be discussed in what order and how meeting time will be distributed. It also makes assignments.

**Good meetings are not likely to happen without a good agenda.**

A good agenda does not guarantee a good meeting, but good meetings are not likely to happen without a good agenda.

My preference is to have any reporting appear early on the agenda since it provides background against which subsequent decisions will be made. Precautions must be taken, however, to prevent reporting from co-opting a disproportionate amount of valuable board meeting time. This can be prevented by distributing the reports in advance. Some boards adopt a consent agenda whereby housekeeping issues like minutes and reports are approved by consent and without discussion unless a director requests otherwise.

## Time management

Good meeting planning requires time management, since time is always limited. The agenda should include a suggested time allotment for each category, if not each agenda item. This helps presenters plan their reports to fit within the time allotted. It also permits everyone in the room to track how the meeting is progressing and accordingly gauge how much airtime they use. Skillful chairpersons protect the decision-making part of the agenda and move the discussion along without appearing to be hurried or heavy-handed.

A major impediment to productive meetings is allowing issues to appear on the agenda before they are ready. I say, "No raw meat! If someone—staff or committee—brings issues that are not ready for board action, consider it raw meat and send it back to the kitchen!"

**No raw meat! If someone brings issues that are not ready for board action, consider it raw meat and send it back to the kitchen!**

CEOs and others who report to the board have not done their duty when they present a problem and conclude by asking, "What shall we do?" They should be required to bring a proposal that discusses the issue and recommends an action for the board to take. (See Exhibit E: Writing Effective Proposals, page 140.)

## Whose rules of order?

All public discourse is governed by rules, but rules must be adapted to the setting. An assembly of several hundred people needs different rules than a small committee.

**I like the sign I saw on the desk of a busy executive in Bogota, Colombia: "No problemas— Soluciones.**

More than 100 years ago, General Henry M. Robert wrote a book on parliamentary law known as *Robert's Rules of Order*. It is based on rules used in the British Parliament, adapted for use by the U.S. Congress. It has become the universally accepted procedure by which meetings are conducted.

*Robert's Rules* provides for an orderly, democratic process. The rules are predicated on the principles that a) the majority has the right to decide; b) the minority has the right to be heard; and c) the rights of absentees need to be protected. The 75th anniversary revised edition lists 44 motions and sets forth the use and function of each.

With due respect for this revered authority, and while affirming the need for order, my conclusion is that strict adherence to *Robert's Rules* is more appropriate for large assemblies like the U.S. Congress, with 435 congressmen and -women competing for limited air time, than for use by small organizations. In a less formal setting, *Robert's* is more likely to intimidate than to facilitate.

*Robert's Rules* has its place, to be sure. There must be order. But for smaller, more informal settings, my preference is to minimize legalism. It is good to be informed by *Robert's* but, I am tempted by the old saying, "This soup we will eat not as hot as it is cooked." More important than if *Robert's Rules* were followed is, did we make good decisions in an atmosphere of mutual respect and collegiality? Do the decisions represent all who were present, and do they own them?

Many things are outside a board's control, but how it does its business—how it conducts its meetings and uses its limited time—is entirely its own doing. The quality of a board's meetings is a measure of its effectiveness. Great boards have great meetings. Great meetings lead the way to organizational greatness.

**Good organizations have good meetings.**

## DISCUSSION QUESTIONS

1. Are your agendas focused on the right issues? Are you using your meeting time well?
2. Does the board docket give you the information needed to do your governance work? Do you have what you need for wise decision-making?

3. Is there a harmonious, trusting, collaborative atmosphere in your boardroom that invites vigorous examination of the issues and alternatives?
4. Is your board making good decisions? Or making no decisions? Are its decisions in the domain of governance and not management (below the line)?
5. Do board committees and the CEO present their recommendations in well-written proposal form for board action? (See Exhibit E: Writing Effective Proposals, page 140.)

# CHAPTER 10

# Consent to Dissent

To get along, you go along. Those famous words come from the Watergate era. They also describe the atmosphere in many boardrooms. Joining a board is like stepping onto a moving train. You are expected to show respect for all that has preceded you and for your fellow directors. In short, you are expected to conform. What's more, resisting takes too much energy. So take the easy course, and enjoy the ride!

How common and how unfortunate. That is how mediocrity gets perpetuated and institutionalized. There is little value in seconding everyone else's motions. Great directors think independently while also being collaborative. They are resolute in finding the best solution to an issue, not bent on finding the quickest compromise.

> **Great directors think independently while also being collaborative.**

## All we like sheep have gone astray

I have never observed it, but I am told that when sheep are released from a corral to pass through a narrow gate, if the first two or three are required to jump over a stick, the rest will jump even after the stick has been removed. How like sheep some boards are. All are jumping in unison to a leader's command.

Often, the chairperson opens the floor for discussion, and immediately a domineering director—most boards have one! —expresses a strong point of view. Not wanting to oppose him or her, everyone falls in line, and soon the chairperson announces a unanimous decision. But is it a good decision? Is it the best option available? The ayes have it, but they aren't always right.

The director who has the courage of conviction and the independence of mind and character to stand up to a gathering majority and present another point of view is invaluable. The best meetings I can recall participating in resulted in a conclusion that emerged from the wisdom of the group after vigorous but disciplined discussion.

## Not all dissent is high-minded

There is a place for dissent, but dissent can also be little more than stubborn negativism. Every action has an underside. Finding it does not require a lot of skill. Most boards have a contrarian in their membership. When someone proposes an initiative, they automatically say no and proceed to humiliate the person who presented it, totally upsetting the boardroom dynamics. It brings to memory the headline to a provocative article, "Welcome to the boardroom, where ideas come to die!" I have been in boardrooms like that.

## Boards must learn to deal with dissent

How does a board deal with dissent and the dissenter? Some lock up when an opposing point of view presents itself, as though some calamity has befallen them. Even to ask a critical question is taboo. I saw one chairman almost literally lose his dentures when his point of view was challenged. My strong advice to chairpersons dealing with pushback is as follows:

1. Don't overreact to dissent. The member is exercising his or her right to be heard. Welcome it.
2. Don't, even in the privacy of your own thoughts, question the dissenter's motive or regard him or her as an enemy or as a trouble maker.
3. Consider objectively and with an open mind the basis for the dissenter's opinion. He or she may prove to be right or at least have a corner of the truth that has not been taken into account adequately.

Quakers, I am told, have a practice of delaying the implementation of a contested decision. Sometimes very basic facts are overlooked in the heat of debate. Delay allows for hindsight and gives another opportunity for collaboration that might take the opposing point of view into account.

While such a practice has some attraction, even one strong-willed member can stall things indefinitely. This can be very trying, and some actions cannot be delayed, but there are times when a pause might be appropriate.

## When in the minority

The question has been called for, the vote has been taken, and you are on the short end. What now? Do you gather up your papers and stalk out of the room while threatening to resign? Do you wait for morning to come before you start telling your friends and anyone who will listen about the stupid decision the board made last night? Perhaps you wait for some months to go by, and when the action encounters difficulty, as many ideas do at mid-point, you announce in a strong voice, "I told you so!"

I know a beautiful story that offers a better approach. A church in Oklahoma had a hard time deciding whether or not to build a new sanctuary. The action was not unanimous, but construction began with members participating in the construction. One morning, six members were shingling the roof. The turnout was disappointing. The weather was unpleasant. During a break, one of the members said, "And to think, I did not even vote for this building." It turned out that none of them had voted for it, and there they were shingling it!

I am not advocating dissent for the sake of dissent. Dissent is not a virtue. It can cause paralyzing gridlock, the likes of which we see too much. I am calling for independent-mindedness that is at the same time collaborative, willing to listen and take another point of view into account.

We really must "reason together." That is what good boardmanship is all about—reasoning together. You may shingle a roof you voted against. You should persist in the search for the best solution available, regardless of who gets the credit.

## DISCUSSION QUESTIONS

1. Is independent thinking encouraged or discouraged on your board? Is it rewarded or punished in your boardroom?
2. Is someone's loyalty or worth questioned if he or she dissents?
3. When is the dissenter expected to concede and support a gathering majority while still retaining his or her conviction and best judgment?

# CHAPTER 11

# Governing Through Policies

The subject of policies has already been introduced, but it is dealt with in this chapter in greater detail. The focus is on policies an organization adopts to do its governance work. Management, it is assumed, has its own policies, which is a subject for another day.

## A policy on policies

Does your board decide each issue on its merit, or do you have a manual of board-approved policies that state your positions on vital topics? This very simple question gets at the heart of an important dimension of board work. The answer has a lot to do with the size and age of the organization. Small, young organizations have few policies and, I might add, many and long meetings. Large organizations usually have a board manual that contains their approved policies.

I think of policy as an instruction to the future, based on experience. When *this* occurs, you are expected or authorized to do *that*. It differs from an ordinary board action that applies to a given situation only. Policy is ongoing until cancelled or amended. Written policies conserve meeting time and increase decision-making consistency.

The board members of a young Habitat affiliate were weary of long meetings. They noted that much meeting time was spent on family selection. Repeatedly, they faced such issues as one-parent families, common-law unions, criminal histories, religious affiliations, or lack thereof, on and on. The board was finally persuaded to draw up a policy stating criteria for family eligibility that took all these variables into account. Thereafter, the Family Selection Committee simply stated that all the families they are recommending comply with the board-approved policy. The board now needs to deal only with exceptions. Their meetings are shorter, and their decisions are better.

## How many policy statements?

Each board must decide where it wants to be on a continuum. At one extreme is policy governance as popularized by John Carver. It establishes a "framework within which to organize the thoughts, activities, structure, and relationships of governing boards." This approach advocates that "all board actions should be governed by a policy." For example, before the board requires a report from the treasurer, it has a policy that states what should be in the report and who should prepare it. That has some advantages. It prevents the reporting format from changing each time there is a new treasurer. But when applied across the entire organization, it can get voluminous and unwieldy.

On the other extreme, there are boards that have no written policies. Everything is decided on its merit as it presents itself. These boards are more nimble, more flexible, but also more inconsistent. My observation is that many boards stay in their pre-policy infancy too long. Many would be served better by promulgating a battery of basic policy statements that will help them in their governance work.

Did you ever wonder why nonprofit directors spend more time in the boardroom than do the directors of large corporations like General

Motors? Part of the answer lies in the fact that corporations work by policy, whereas nonprofits' boards have a tendency to fall below the Big X line and end up spending time in management issues. As a venture grows, it is necessary for the board to ease up on the hands-on stuff that it so much enjoys and make the transition into policy governance.

## Steps in the utilization of policies

Policy statements are useful only if they are readily available when needed. This suggests that they should be filed in a well-indexed Policy Manual. The following questions may help you decide if more attention should be given to introducing or expanding a policy manual:

- What are the issues that appear on your agenda with some regularity and use up a lot of meeting time?
- What are the values and practices that you want to preserve? Here is an opportunity for a sitting board to condense what they have learned and pass it on to their successors. This prevents reinventing the wheel.

## Policies are servants, not masters

There is danger in either extreme. Too few written policies leaves too much to the discretion of the moment. On the other extreme, neither do you want to becomes Moses the lawgiver. Too many policies make an organization muscle-bound. I don't know which extreme is worse. This is a balance each organization must find on its own, and it will change as the organization grows. In all of this, it is important to remember that policies are servant, not master. They are meant to serve us. We don't serve them.

My advice is for a medium-sized organization to make a modest beginning of maybe ten or twelve basic policies, covering the most critical areas. Then add policies as the need for them arises. Bear in mind, however, that this is a board governance exercise. Avoid crossing over the Big X line and getting into management. Management presumably has its own set of administrative policies.

One policy that would surely be in any board manual would state that all issues requiring board action should be presented in proposal form as shown in Exhibit E, page 140.

## Status of policies

Once agreed to and filed in the policy book, policies should not be looked upon as being the law of the Medes and the Persians (or unchangeable). There are three things directors can do with approved policies other than strict adherence, when that appears to be called for.

1. Policies can be set aside. Maybe there are unique circumstances that were not anticipated when a policy was approved. It is permissible to set it aside while retaining it for future use.
2. Policies can be amended to take new and changed circumstances into account.
3. Policies should be reviewed periodically and retired when they no longer serve a useful purpose. They are yours to do with as you see fit.

Just one further word of warning. While willingness to approve changes can be a sign of maturity, in the extreme it can also lead to fickleness. The framers of the United States Constitution wisely set a very high standard for any changes.

## A policy manual is a working document

The board policy manual should be distributed to all board members and senior staff. It should be included in the new director kit. It is meant to be an in-house document, not highly confidential but also not intended for public distribution. Someone should be appointed to keep it current, perhaps the board secretary or vice president. It is part of growing up. It becomes an important part of your virtual Global Positioning System.

## DISCUSSION QUESTIONS

1. Does your board have written policies that are appropriate to your size, or do you decide issues on their merit as they arise? Should you have more written policies?

2. Does your board have a policy manual where all approved governance policies are readily available for consultation on a timely basis? If it doesn't, should it?

3. Has someone been assigned to keep the board policy manual current—that is, to remove policies that are no longer relevant? To add new policies as they are adopted? Are copies of the manual available to all board members?

# CHAPTER 12

# Boardroom Behavior

**W**herever two or three are gathered, there will be differences. Well-intended people may look at the same facts and arrive at different conclusions. This need not be bad. Differences exist only where there are multiple options, and options are good. They can be signs of life, of energy.

> **Differences exist only where there are multiple options, and options are good.**

Boardrooms should be greenhouses filled with new life, not graveyards. An absence of differences may, in fact, be attributed to lethargy, indifference, or stifled creativity. Any of these are many times worse than differences.

The issue, therefore, is not differences. The issue is what happens when differences morph into conflict. Conflict may be the phase through which some differences pass en route to resolution. But do these differences *pass through*? That is, do they get resolved, or do they become permanently embedded, only to resurface in an even more virile form later? It is unquestioningly healthier and more constructive to deal with conflict openly, rather than denying it, driving it under the table, or wishing it away.

In dealing with differences constructively, it is useful to understand the behavioral styles that repeatedly play out in boardrooms.

**Competing** directors are intent upon winning—every time! They ignore, deny, or even manipulate facts that do not support their predetermined conclusions. They place a low value on discussion and group process. Their competitive style is individualistic and intimidating. They resort to whatever it takes to prevail.

**Accommodating** directors support the prevailing point of view. In their eagerness to be liked by everyone, they are quick to agree with whatever solution is emerging, whether it is the best option or not. They invariably agree with the last person who spoke. Accommodators always vote with the majority.

**Avoiding** directors are uncomfortable with any divergent point of view. Their first objective, therefore, is not to arrive at the *best* conclusion but to stay out of the crossfire of anything resembling a disagreement. Even a differing point of view is uncomfortable for them. When the discussion heats up, they shut down.

**Compromising** directors are skillful at gathering together several points of view on which there appears to be agreement, and then cobbling together a compromised solution. This may appear on the surface to be helpful, but too often it turns out to be shallow, and therefore temporary. Instead of holding out for the best solution, compromisers can pull the discussion to the lowest common denominator.

**Collaborating** directors welcome alternative points of view. They weigh each alternative on its merit objectively. Collaborators willingly risk divergent points of view in their search for the *best* solution. They are not much interested in who wins and who loses. Because collaborators arrive at a conclusion collectively, they also own it collectively and work at making it work.

The first four behaviors are driven by self-interest: How can I win? How can I be liked? How can I avoid being embarrassed? How can I be the hero? They arise from the false self. By way of comparison, the collaborator's first concern is to arrive at the best solution. His or her strongest motive is to draw the best from the group. Boards that work in a collaborative atmosphere are fortunate—and more effective.

## Dealing with contrarians

There is yet another behavioral style—the contrarian. Contrarians fixate on the underside of an idea. Whatever is proposed, the contrarian prefers the opposite. If the consensus is black, the contrarian extols white and identifies everything wrong with black.

Contrarians are not bothered by being in the minority. Some enjoy it. It gets them attention and makes them feel powerful. They may be disruptive, but even avowed contrarians deserve to be heard. They usually have a point, and on occasion they may even be right.

The challenge that faces every board, and particularly the chairperson, is to create a collegial environment where turf and ego considerations are sublimated to seeking the highest common good. This requires trust among the members and a willingness to be vulnerable. It calls for independence of thought and the self-confidence to be differentiated.

Two senior churchmen had a sharp disagreement. When adjournment time came, one of the disputants asked the other to offer a closing prayer. He rose to the occasion admirably. I do not remember the exact words, but the prayer included the memorable line, "Thank you for those who disagree with us. They help us to think thoughts we might not otherwise think." And so they do.

## Debilitating conflict

The presumption to this point has been that the conflict is within the ability of the board to resolve on its own. It is also assumed that the grievance procedure, which every organization should have, has been utilized. This is where conflict resolution should begin. But there are sometimes hurts and conflicts that are beyond a board's ability to resolve.

The temptation is to ignore the conflict and pretend that it does not exist. That may make it worse. "Time," it is said, "heals all wounds." My experience suggests the substitution of one word: Time heals *some* wounds. Sometimes the conflict is so debilitating that the time for healing is exhausted before the dispute is resolved.

**Ignoring a conflict may make it worse.**

At this stage, it is necessary to determine if the conflict centers on one person or if it penetrates deeply into the board and maybe the entire organization. If it is the former, it needs to be addressed with that individual. Conciliation services are available, and many disputes are resolved at that level. In extreme cases, it may be necessary to dismiss the individual, to get the wrong people off the bus, as Jim Collins says. However, even that should be done in a conciliatory fashion, acknowledging that the board may have contributed in some way. Organizational admissions of wrongdoing are too rare.

If the conflict is more systemic in nature and is threatening to render your board or the entire organization dysfunctional, and if all reasonable efforts have been exhausted, it may be time to invite professional help. In doing so, the board must step over two huge obstacles: cost and the fear that it will be seen as weak or unstable.

**The hidden cost of an unresolved, protracted dispute can be enormous.**

As far as cost is concerned, the hidden cost of an unresolved, protracted dispute can be enormous and far exceed the charges for professional assistance. The fear of damage to the organization's reputation is a mixed bag. Some may regard it negatively, while others will respect you for dealing with a difficult issue. Never let fear stop you from doing the right thing.

In all this, we are challenged to practice the Golden Rule: "Do unto others as you would have them do unto you."

## DISCUSSION QUESTIONS

1. Does your board have the ability to deal with differences constructively, or are differences allowed to accumulate and morph into debilitating conflict?
2. When conflict rears its ugly head, does your board deal with it openly, or is it left to drain your energy and joy? How skillful is your board in collaborating its way to the best solution?
3. Does your board have conflicts now that need to be resolved?
4. How do you regard someone who sees things differently? Are such persons valued, or is their usefulness questioned?

# CHAPTER 13

# The Role of the Chairperson

There is more to chairing a board than sitting at the prestigious end of a large table, deftly glad-handing your way through an agenda someone else has prepared.

I was conducting a one-day workshop for a board when I saw the newly elected chairperson sitting with that deer-in-the-headlights look. At break time he said to me, "I had no idea what I was getting myself into." Later I said to myself, "I wonder how many chairpersons feel that way? Worse yet, how many people sit in the chair without knowing all that the job entails?"

Did you ever wonder where that nondescript term "the chair" comes from? It dates back to a time when the only chair in the room was for the presiding officer. And since that person was always, until recently, a male, he was called the chair*man*. Now that has changed to chairperson, or just the "chair" since the position may be filled by a female.

The role of the chair is one of the least prescribed of any within an organization. Her/his microphone is always open. Each chairperson defines the office to suit him- or herself—to a point. At best, the chairperson is servant of all.

## The chairperson's role as presider of meetings

It is commonly understood that chairpersons preside over meetings. S/he serves as host of the meeting, making everyone feel welcome and creating a collegial meeting atmosphere. S/he takes care to distribute the available time across the entire agenda, including the items that appear at the end of the agenda.

The real skill is in accomplishing this without appearing to be heavy-handed or hurried. If you would not want to be the second verse in a song when the meeting is running late, you would not want to be the last agenda item with an ineffective chair.

Few things frustrate me more than what I call meeting drift. An unassertive or incompetent chairperson allows the discussion to bounce around indiscriminately like a game of Ping-Pong. While processing one issue, a second issue is introduced. The two chase each other around on the board table like two playful puppies with no more result. The effective chairperson keeps the discussion focused on the single issue under consideration. If I am chairing and the discussion is prolonged, I may remind the board of the hour and what still remains on the agenda. I may also question if tabling may be an option. Discussion should not be permitted to go on indefinitely.

> **The effective chairperson keeps the discussion focused on a single issue at a time.**

I was once criticized for having sneaked a look at my watch while a prolonged discussion was underway. It seemed distracting to the person who objected, perhaps intimidating. My first impulse was to cry, "Cheap shot! After all, you expect me as chair to adjourn the meeting on time." Then a better thought occurred to me: Sure, I needed to keep track of time, but I could do it less conspicuously. Thereafter I placed my watch on the table so I could check it without being noticed. At least I hadn't shaken my watch to see if it was still running.

## The chairperson's non-meeting role

Although less public than chairing, the chairperson's second role pertains to the time between board meetings. This function is probably as important as presiding over meetings, although less understood and less defined.

First among the chairperson's non-meeting responsibilities is interacting with and supporting the CEO. The effective CEO supports his or her staff. The board, through the chairperson, supports the CEO. A respectful relationship between the chair and the CEO, two of the most important offices in any organization, is of paramount importance. There cannot be conflict at this level without dire consequences.

A distinction I have found helpful is that the chairperson is responsible for how the *board* functions (above the Big X line), while operations (below the Big X line) are under the direction of the CEO. Making this distinction in practice is not always easy, but it stands as a useful guiding principle.

Another non-meeting duty of a chair is to represent the board when it is not in session. In so doing, the chair must be careful not to usurp the authority of the board and to keep the board well informed when acting on its behalf.

The chairperson, in consultation with the CEO, also appoints standing committees and helps to coordinate their activities. Much business comes to the board through the committees. Unless committees are well directed, they may overlap with each other or get into operations. They sometimes bump into each other, run over staff, or get into the CEO's hair. The chairperson has a role in keeping this energy well directed.

As already suggested, the chairperson participates with the CEO in drawing up board meeting agendas. This involves being in communication with committee chairs to identify the issues that are ready for board action. Issues not adequately precooked should not be allowed to appear on the agenda. When this discipline is not practiced, a board finds itself chewing on half-cooked meat.

Finally, a good chair finds ways to provide meaningful involvement for the vice chair, assuming there is one.

When I was chairman of Habitat, I occasionally made a visit to the headquarters between meetings to consult with Millard Fuller, then the CEO, to ensure good coordination between the board and management. On occasion, staff members asked to meet with me. I was on the spot. I knew such meetings had the potential to compromise the oft referred to Big X line separating governance from operations. But declining to make myself available to meet also said something I did not like.

I resolved it by agreeing to meet, but with the clear understanding that while I would hear them, any action resulting from our conversation would need to go through the established line of authority. It was not always easy to know where that line was, since in some cases it involved confidentialities, but we managed, in part because we knew our respective roles.

## A reminder to chairpersons

While the chair sits at the top of the organizational pyramid, s/he is also accountable. As stated so poignantly by Robert Greenleaf, "No one, *absolutely no one*, is to be entrusted with the operational use of power without the close oversight of fully functioning trustees." The chair is accountable first to the board and ultimately to the membership.

President Lyndon Johnson, not the humblest of men, said upon leaving office, "The presidency has made every man who occupied it, no matter how small, bigger than he was, and no matter how big, not big enough for its demands." That puts chairing into perspective.

So a reminder to chairpersons—you are expected to lead, not dominate. You are expected to hear everyone, whether you agree with him or her or not. You are expected to help the board or committee find a way, not insist that it must be your way. In so doing, it is good to look over your shoulder occasionally to see who, if anyone, is following.

## DISCUSSION QUESTIONS

1. Is there a time when the directors on your board are invited to make suggestions about how board meetings are conducted?
2. Are your chair and CEO in good communication with each other?
3. Is there a time when directors are invited to make suggestions about how the chairperson represents the board when it is not in session?
4. Are there ways that you as board members could help the chairperson with her or his function?
5. When was the last time you thanked your chairperson?

# CHAPTER 14

# The Minute Record

The role of the recording secretary is one of the least sought-after positions on any board or committee. Yet it is one of the most important. If the agenda contains what business will be dealt with in a meeting, the minutes record for posterity what transpired.

The approval of minutes is often done so perfunctorily, it leaves the impression that minutes are a mere formality, some might even say a nuisance. Not so.

## Minutes have four functions

Minutes should be written with the following purposes in mind:

1. Legal: The first thing a lawyer requests in a legal proceeding is the minute record.
2. Authorization: Minutes are the official basis by which an action is authorized.

3. Informational: Minutes provide information for absent members and others with a right to know.
4. Historical record: Minutes preserve what was done for future examination.

## Desired length/detail

Some minutes are, in my opinion, too detailed, while others are too brief. When minutes are too detailed, the temptation is to ignore them. Minutes should, without fail, record official actions accurately.

> **Minutes should record official actions accurately.**

If a motion or an action is not clear, the recording secretary should not hesitate to stop and ask the chair for clarification. Sometimes the mover is asked to present the motion in writing.

If the minute record is too skimpy and includes only the official motions or actions with no mention of discussion, the context is lost. For historical purposes, the minute record should include a one-or two-paragraph summary of what led to a major decision. Years later, it will help anyone to see not only what was done, but why.

I do not like minutes to have a lot of verbatim dialogue. Cut the "he said, she said" details from the record. It is boring to have to listen to that in a meeting, much less having to read it in the minutes. The needle has a way of getting lost in the haystack.

My practice, and I have written many minutes, is to make extensive use of attachments.

That is, the official action is stated in the minutes with reference to an attachment where additional details can be found. This shortens the body of the minutes and increases authenticity. The original document, not a second-hand summary, goes forward for future examination.

## Who records the minutes?

This function is normally assigned to the board secretary in the bylaws. In practice, at least in organizations with a professional staff, minute-taking is often assigned to a staff person. This frees the secretary to participate in board deliberation, but it also leaves me with a little disquietude. Think about it. This action assigns an all-important, above-the-line governance function to a below-the-line staff person. It cedes to a staff person the authority to, in effect, choose the language by which a board action will be recorded.

Ultimately, I forego an objection if the staff recorder and the board secretary collaborate on the final minutes before they are released for board approval. Having a staff person record the minutes does not change the fact that the secretary remains legally responsible for the minute record.

**The secretary remains legally responsible for the minute record.**

In the distribution of minutes, attachments are included only for the official minute book and for persons not in attendance, since those in attendance already have them in the meeting docket.

## Minute approval

Some organizations have the practice of submitting a draft of the minutes to the board chair before releasing them. That has its advantages if it does not result in undue delay. It is important to remember that minutes are official only after the board approves them at the next meeting.

## Prompt release of minutes

Minutes, I feel strongly, must be available within days of a meeting, at least in draft form. This is especially true for boards that meet monthly. Minutes are never easier to write than immediately after a meeting. How else is management, or anyone else charged with following up

**Minutes are never easier to write than immediately after a meeting.**

a meeting, going to know precisely what was authorized? The value of a meeting is diminished appreciatively by a long delay in circulating the minutes and by minutes that are carelessly recorded.

## Freedom to interpret

How much freedom does the recorder have to interpret what was said and concluded? The short answer: Not much. Minutes must be, as much as humanly possible, the complete, true, and accurate record of what transpired at a meeting. A good recording secretary can make a chaotic meeting look more orderly than it was, but the recorder is *never* entitled to change the meaning of what transpired. Careless chairing makes minute-taking difficult.

## Written proposals

Minutes are easier to write when major issues are presented in proposal form, complete with an actionable recommendation that states the action being requested. (For a model, see Exhibit E: Writing Effective Proposals, page 140.) This greatly facilitates recording and improves accuracy. I consider it a coup when a recommendation I have written is approved as presented and read right into the minute record. It should be clear, however, that the board is not obligated to give *carte blanche* approval to a recommendation. It has the right to amend and even disapprove as it sees fit.

A meeting is not complete until the minutes are written and approved at the next meeting. They are the official record of what transpired.

## Circulation of minutes

Organizations with a widely scattered membership sometimes use meeting minutes to inform persons not in a meeting but with a right to know. That has obvious advantages, but again with a downside. When minutes are widely circulated, there is a tendency to record sensitive and perhaps confidential information in more general terms. I know of instances where information got into the public domain prematurely through minutes. My own preference is to hold minutes rather close and use other means to inform those with a right to know.

My hope is that this discussion has given you an opportunity to re-think how you are attending to your minute record. It is an important part of your organizational stewardship.

## DISCUSSION QUESTIONS

1. Are your board meeting minutes available within one week of a meeting? Do you read them?
2. Do the minutes record what was discussed and concluded at a meeting, and do they fulfill the four purposes stated in this chapter?
3. Can the secretary confirm that the official minute book is current and complete with significant attachments? Is it kept in a fireproof vault or file? Remember that it is the official memory of your organization.

# CHAPTER 15

# The Board Role in Fundraising

"**A**ccording to your faith, let it be done to you," states the Bible. Nonprofits might paraphrase this to say, "According to your *fundraising*, let it be done to you." The simple, undeniable fact is that the scale of a nonprofit's activity is determined by its ability to raise funds, whether by charging for services or by public appeals.

## The role of directors in fundraising

Fund solicitation expectations are among the activities many directors detest. Some even decline board service for that reason. At the same time, getting directors to be more active in fundraising ranks among the strongest desire CEOs have for their boards. Some organizations stack their boards with deep pockets, hoping to raise as much as 40% of their annual budget from the board. That is fine as long as deep pockets don't become the main criteria in the selection of directors. Deep pockets alone do not make a good governing board.

I heard Millard Fuller say to the Habitat board on more than one occasion, "If you are not the most dynamic and energetic fundraiser, give your chair to someone who will," or words to that effect. It did not endear him to the board, but it got our attention.

Let's be clear, the board's first responsibility is above the line. It is to put in place a system that will ensure that the resources are available to complete the approved plan. It is also reasonable to expect that, before directors ask others to contribute, they will themselves have contributed in proportion to their ability. Directors need to find their place in raising the money needed to float the program they approve. This is especially true of small or young organizations who have limited staff.

> **A database of active and potential donors is as valuable as a bank account.**

Directors who are shy about solicitation, or are not gifted in doing so, can participate in one or all of the following ways:

- By introducing the cause to their friends who are potential contributors. A database of active and potential donors is more valuable than a bank account.
- By accompanying other directors or professional fundraisers who do the asking. The presence of a director, even when silent, speaks volumes to a potential donor. I have even seen directors become comfortable doing their own solicitation after first accompanying someone else. Some boards use a buddy system.
- By thanking contributors. It has been said that a contributor has not been thanked until he or she has been thanked five times. I personally do not want to be thanked five times. I am more inclined to say donors should be thanked in ways that leave them feeling *appropriately* thanked. That will vary. Some contributors want anonymity while others expect plaques. When people are appropriately thanked, they are more likely to give again, and maybe even increase the size of their gifts. Even timid directors

can be enjoyably engaged in thanking donors. It may be as simple as making a phone call, sending a thank you note, or hosting someone for coffee at Starbucks.

- By volunteering to help with fundraising events. In so doing, remember that this is a volunteer role, not a board role. You are responsible to whoever is in charge, be that a board member or staff.

I have observed that when directors (and employees) are too far removed from the source of funds, they have a tendency to get careless about the value of money.

## A more in-depth understanding of fundraising

Some directors resist fundraising because they view it as begging. Fundraising is secondarily about raising money. It is first about *raising friends* for the cause. Many people are looking for an opportunity to support something they can believe in. They want to make a difference somewhere. Helping such philanthropic individuals find a match for their charitable giving can be a valuable and deeply satisfying experience.

> **Fundraising is about raising friends for the cause.**

You are also doing someone a huge favor when you help to liberate him or her from crass materialism and narcissism and steer that person to a life of giving. John David Mann and Bob Burg illustrate this beautifully in the little gem, *The Go-Giver*. You might consider giving a book like this to all the members of your board, both as a gift for their work and to give them a fuller understanding of fund/friendraising.

## Prerequisites for effective fundraising

To be effective, directors, and all fundraisers, need to be supplied with the following:

1. Before launching into a major campaign, take a hard, objective look at the case you are trying to "sell." Is it appealing? Urgent? Well presented?

   Covering a deficit or soliciting for something that has already happened (like a building that is already built) does not appeal. The prospective donor wants above all else to be convinced that his or her contribution will make life better for someone. Nothing is as appealing as a record of performance.

2. Be clear about how much money you are attempting to raise from different categories, such as foundations, major donors, or government sources. Professional fundraisers always have a goal in mind, not only for the campaign but for each person they are soliciting. Do not be shy about asking.

3. Arrange a matching grant. They add appeal.

4. Make a multi-year appeal. Your request should ask for a gift now as well as a pledge to be paid in future years. The advantages are obvious, yet few do it. You will need money next year as well, and the next. It should lay the groundwork for the next year(s). Make sure the pledge is recorded and followed up on.

5. Have an understanding about who solicits whom to avoid meeting a fellow director in some major donor's revolving door! Make sure major donors are matched with the solicitor who has the most meaningful connection to her/him. Unskilled solicitors leave a lot of money on the table.

6. Precede the campaign with a well-planned public announcement. Get someone to write a timely feature article combined with a paid ad. Remember, it takes money to raise money.

7. Have printed material available to support the solicitation effort. It does not need to be slick, but it needs to be informative and inviting.

8. Know whom you are soliciting. Do your homework. A wealth of information is available from Google and other public sources. If possible, ask someone who may be a friend of the person being solicited to accompany you.

Inviting a professional fundraiser to coach your board can also increase the effectiveness and confidence of amateur fundraisers.

> **It takes money to raise money.**

Some organizations name prestigious chairpersons to increase public appeal. Habitat has surely benefited enormously from the generous endorsement of former U.S. President Jimmy Carter. Both Jimmy and Rosalynn Carter have few equals, but bear in mind, they are effective because they are authentic. When I am asked, "What do you talk with the President about while on a build?" my answer is "You don't. Carter always says, "This is no photo op. I came to build and I assume you did, too."

So, directors, pull up your socks and go to work. Find your place in raising the money needed to fund the projects you approve.

## DISCUSSION QUESTIONS

1. Are the members of your board adequately involved in fundraising?
2. Are board members supplied with publicity materials and manageable assignments to perform productively?
3. Could/should more be done to equip and coach board members to increase their fundraising confidence and effectiveness?

# CHAPTER 16

# Board Committees— Getting More with Less

Committees are a vital part of many organizations. Many could not exist without committees. They help boards with their above-the-Big-X-line governance task by:

- lightening up the agenda;
- giving greater attention to specialized subjects like finance;
- providing members of the board with the opportunity for increased participation.

Committees are even more essential for organizations that do not have a CEO, since committees fill both the governance and the program implementation roles. This would include such community mainstay organizations as Parent Teacher Organizations, music and athletic groups, service clubs, and on and on.

## Cautions about committees

For all their virtues, however, committees have downsides that need to be recognized so they can be avoided.

When John Carver was asked how many standing committees a board should have (for its governance function), he surprised everyone by saying, "None." None?! His reasoning is instructive. A board's role encompasses the entire organization. Committees, to use his term, "distract from board wholeness." They dissect the organization into functional parts, and in that process, the wholeness that needs to characterize the organization is lost.

> **Committees can dissect the wholeness that needs to characterize an organization.**

This is harsh enough, but there is more. Board committees have a tendency, if allowed, to take on lives of their own. They assume authority that was never intended, including usurping the role of the board. Each committee has a part of the action, but only the board sees the entire picture. Board committees can be pictured as a series of huge silos (the individual committees) operating under a thin umbrella (the board). While I served on the board of Habitat, committee meetings took up more board member time than board meetings.

Yet another problem with board committees is that they, even more than the board itself, have a tendency to go below the Big X line and end up doing staff work instead of governance. The line, for example, between the board treasurer, who often also serves as the chairperson of the finance committee, and the CFO is hard to distinguish. In too many cases, the treasurer ends up focusing more on management than governance issues.

> **Committees are not necessarily always an efficient use of time.**

Making matters worse, in the process, the role of the CEO is often bypassed or invaded.

Nor is the extensive use of board committees as efficient as is sometimes thought. The board assigns an issue to a committee. The committee then reaches its conclusion and recommends it back to the board. If the board "digs deep," it is re-doing the work that the committee had already done. If the board approves it routinely, it is being superficial. All this is using up the directors' time when, in many cases, it would have been better if the board had dealt with it as a committee of the whole in the first place.

Sometimes a board resorts to appointing a committee because they want to duck a complicated and controversial issue. There are times when that serves a good purpose, but there are also times when the board is just seeking the easy way out.

> **I chaired a board that had a program committee and a finance committee that met simultaneously. The program committee, predictably, recommended the approval of a new exciting program. The finance committee, not knowing what the program committee had concluded, projected a year-end deficit and recommended a budget freeze. The two committees cancelled each other out, leaving the final decision to the board.**

## A minimalist approach

Putting the pros and cons on the scale, I suggest a four-point minimalist approach.

1. **No more committees than necessary.** It is hard to be specific without being arbitrary. My suggestion is that an organization might start with just three standing committees and then add committees as suggested by experience.

   - Board Service Committee: It evaluates how the individual directors are performing and how they are functioning collectively as a board. It also keeps the board strong by having vetted directors ready to step in when vacancies occur.
   - Finance Committee: It exercises fiduciary responsibility in the important and complex financial area, including oversight of the annual audit (which is addressed to the board, not management) and any resulting recommendations.
   - Futures Committee: The natural tendency is for boards to be so focused on the here and now that a special committee is needed to give this—one of a board's most important functions—the attention it deserves.

Note the absence of a program committee. Program is so close to the heart of an organization that the board should deal with it directly and not via a committee.

What about an Executive Committee? If I were to design a model governance for an intermediate sized organization, it would have no more than twelve directors, preferably nine, and no Executive Committee. An Executive Committee sets up two classes of board membership. Unless extreme discipline is exercised, the Executive Committee usurps the role intended for the board. It diminishes the role of the directors who are not on the Executive Committee. It also results in duplication of effort as observed above.

There must always be room for exceptions. Large organizations with diverse and geographically scattered constituencies may feel compelled to seat a large board, and in such cases, an Executive Committee becomes necessary. It should consist of the officers and other members but not exceed one-third of the board membership in size.

> **If nonprofits had to pay for committee time, they would use it more sparingly.**

2. **No larger than necessary.** Up to five committee members is manageable; seven is the maximum. But a committee should never exceed one-third of the board membership. Even a committee of two will do. I once served on a committee of one and enjoyed it immensely! If nonprofits had to pay for committee time, they would use it more sparingly.

3. **Meet no more often than necessary.** Many committee meetings are longer and more frequent than necessary because they do not observe the rule of completed staff and/or committee work. My mantra of "no raw meat" applies to committee meetings as well as board meetings.

   Instead of asking the committee to start its deliberation from scratch, the committee chair brings (better yet, distributes in advance) a draft that already makes a start on the assignment. It identifies the options and tests a conclusion. This procedure facilitates the meeting and still allows for member participation. It calls for the exercise of leadership.

> **If a meeting is well planned, two hours should accomplish what the committee is capable of doing.**

4. **Meet no longer than necessary.** I deny it, but I am quoted as having said that the Holy Spirit does not stick around after about 9:30 or 10:00 p.m. If a meeting is well planned and presided over, the first two hours will accomplish what the committee is capable of in that sitting.

In fact, who said meetings must last two hours? You know the old rule: the amount of time required to do something expands to the amount allotted. I have had good success with what I call stand-up meetings for one-item agendas, giving new meaning to the term *standing committees*. Most of our meeting rooms, I insist, are too comfortable. Meetings would be shorter if conference rooms had no chairs, guaranteed.

## Appointment of committees

The chairperson of the board appoints all standing committees annually. They have a written job description that states what they are expected to accomplish. They understand that they have only the authority ceded to them by the board. Only when authorized do they act on behalf of the board. They report to the board regularly. Any recommendations requiring board action should be presented in proposal form and be available days before the board meeting where action is expected.

The chairperson and CEO are ex officio members of all standing committees except the Board Service Committee. (They do not serve on the BSC because their work, too, is being reviewed.) They may not attend all meetings, but they get the minutes and make sure they are in the loop.

Task forces are distinguished from standing committees. Whereas standing committees are meant to be ongoing, task forces exist for a defined function. When **Task forces exist for a defined function.** that task is completed, the task force is dissolved. The judicial use of task forces is, in the minds of some, associated with high-performing organizations.

The subject of committees is summarized in the title of this chapter—getting more with less. Boards get better results when they use committees sparingly and for a defined purpose.

# DISCUSSION QUESTIONS

1. Do your board committees understand that they have only the authority assigned to them by the board? Do they know that they do not act for the board, but prepare issues for board action?
2. Does your board have enough committees? Too many? The right committees?
3. Do your board committees have current job descriptions?
4. Do they present their findings in actionable form?
5. Do they keep the board well informed?

# CHAPTER 17

# Budget—A Necessary Management Tool

The word "budget" is not viewed favorably by many people. A budget is, in my experience, not only useful; it is a necessary tool for both board and management.

## The function of budgets and budgeting

A well prepared budget is an essential planning instrument. Budgeting *is* financial planning. An organization that does not have a budget is not planning. It is that simple. Budgets help to anticipate

> **An organization that does not have a budget is not planning.**

income and expenses. This makes it possible to foresee if resources will be adequate to complete the plan and avoids running out of gas before year's end.

The *process* of budgeting can be as valuable as the resulting budget. A budget permits you to examine the individual line items and consciously assess their cost-effectiveness. Budgeting allows you to compare projected financial activity with previous years, permitting you to observe trends. Gross sales/income may be going up, but expenses may be going up faster, resulting in a deficit. Budgeting helps management anticipate trends and make adjustments accordingly.

The budget also helps directors and managers to see how resources are distributed and to ensure that this is in accordance with the board approved mission. There is always the possibility of an organization saying one thing and doing another—without even knowing it. A careful reading of the budget reveals an organization's true priorities. You can tell much about an organization by reading its budget.

> **A careful reading of the budget reveals an organization's true priorities.**

Finally, a budget is an efficient way for a board to authorize staff on financial matters. If an activity is included within an approved budget, the funds are considered to be authorized. With an approved budget in place, management only needs to seek approval for a new program activity in the course of the year. This greatly facilitates decision-making by the board and frees it for more productive work. It also underscores the need for boards to enter deeply into the budget-building process. It is the process by which their resources are being distributed.

By way of contrast, the manager of an organization that does not have a budget must come to the board for authorization for practically all actions with financial implications. This is unnecessarily time-consuming and demeaning to the manager. A budget defines the financial parameters within which the manager is authorized to operate.

## An illustration of how it works

When I was in charge of the Mennonite Central Committee's multi-million-dollar overseas program reaching into fifty countries, the annual planning process began by arriving at an understanding with the Executive Committee about how much money would be available for programming. This was usually expressed in a percentage up or down from the current budget. The Executive Committee also had the opportunity to influence program content by suggesting categories that should be increased or decreased in the recommended plan.

Once that macro figure was established, staff was authorized to prepare a budget draft that distributed the anticipated funds to the respective continental areas according to the agreed-upon program priorities and needs. Next, continental directors worked with individual country directors to draw up their annual program plans within the suggested budget.

These plans/budgets then worked their way up though the chain of command (we used more democratic language) with final authorization coming from the board in its annual meeting. It was truly a participatory process. Each of the five levels of administration understood and performed its role within the larger scheme. The ultimate test? It worked! Rapport and trust between the board and operations were strong. If our plan had a weakness, it was that we did not give enough attention to defining the ultimate endgame of the individual programs. We were too inclined to continue down the old tracks.

## Arriving at the best budgeting procedure

There is no one prescribed format that works for everyone; at least I have not found it.

Every organization must devise its own format. The real value of budgeting normally becomes apparent only after the second or third year, when meaningful comparisons are possible. Some experimentation may be required before arriving at the format that will serve you best. When budgets are too detailed, they become cumbersome, making

> **The real value of budgeting usually becomes apparent only after the second or third year.**

skeptics question if they are worth the bother. When they are too brief, they fail to serve their purpose. The challenge is to get started and then adjust as experience suggests.

## Two practical tips in closing

I like to work with a spreadsheet that has four columns: current year experience, current year budget, previous year experience, and previous year recommended budget. In some categories, you might also add a fifth year experience, giving you a longer financial history. Much valuable financial information can be condensed on one page using this format.

Second, I learned by experience the shortsightedness of committing 100 percent of the anticipated income to line items in the annual budget. In a dynamic organization, there will always be new challenges that present themselves in the course of the year. Some budget overruns are inevitable. Do yourself a favor. Reserve a substantial amount (maybe as much as 10 percent of the budget) for miscellaneous and unforeseen expenses and resist the temptation to surrender it in a difficult budget-balancing year. That gives you some flexibility and the ability to respond to challenges that present themselves throughout the year.

A well designed budget is your friend, not your master. It is an instrument that helps you match your money to your plans.

# DISCUSSION QUESTIONS

1. Does your board have an annual line item budget format that distributes your available funds in accordance with your priorities?

2. Is your board supplied with financial reporting that permits you to track income and expenditures against the approved budget, with comparisons to the previous year?

3. Is there provision in your budget to respond to needs and unexpected expenses that arise in the course of the year?

4. Do you have a clear understanding with management regarding its authorization in regard to finances?

5. Are you well served by the financial reporting and budgeting format now in use?

## CHAPTER 18

# Helping Directors Become Great Leaders

This chapter is intended for all directors and senior staff, not just the chair and the CEO. You are all leaders, showing the way to a better future, exercising your God-given abilities in the places where you move and have your being.

"Lead, follow, or get out of the way," said Thomas Paine. The world waits to be well led. In all endeavors—congregations, orchestras, corporations, athletic teams—leadership is key.

**The capacity to lead people is among the most sought-after and rewarded human abilities.**

Leadership is a complex subject. It is filled with intangibles and ambiguities, but amid them there are some universal principles that characterize great leadership.

1. Leadership is about leading *people*. Unlike technicians who master their trades, leaders specialize in giving direction to and motivating people. Great leaders are not those who are able to do the work of two or even ten, but they are those who are able to lead an effort involving thousands. The capacity to lead people is among the most sought-after and rewarded human abilities.

2. The first responsibility of a leader, says Max De Pree, is to define reality. Leaders accept the present as their starting point. Rudy Giuliani was elected mayor of New York City when it was said to be an unmanageable city. He did not have the luxury of imagining New York as some idyllic middle class suburb. He accepted New York as it was and proceeded to rehabilitate it with visible results.

3. The best leaders are service driven, not power driven. Leaders by definition have power, but they are most effective when they use it to empower others. Tom Peters states, "Leaders don't create followers, they create more leaders."

4. Great leaders have high intellectual and physical energy. Energy comes from passion, vision, and an optimistic spirit. A leader simply cannot be lethargic or have a pessimistic spirit. It is a contradiction. Leadership requires people who are able to see and believe in things before they exist. That is energy-producing.

5. Leadership is by definition about effecting change. To do this, the leader must overcome a mentality that wants to stay put. A leader must be bold and ready to trade the present, with which it is comfortable, for something that has the potential to be better, but which has not yet had an opportunity to prove its merit. Managing change successfully is a leader's greatest challenge.

6. Great leaders are risk-takers. Leadership involves navigating where there is no map and sometimes even no road. It involves putting trust in people and ideas before they have proven themselves. The challenge is stated eloquently by George Bernard Shaw: "You see things, and you say, 'Why?' But I dream things that never were; and I say, 'Why not?'"

7. Leaders must be well matched to their tasks. Even a strong leader fails when placed in a role for which he or she is not well suited. A large, established nonprofit requires different leadership skills than an infant organization. Managing a thrift store requires different management skills than managing a high-end jewelry store.

8. Great leaders engender trust. They are themselves trustworthy. This requires them to be transparent and, to quote Jack Welch in *Winning*, they "can't have an iota of fakeness." People will not follow, nor will they put out for, someone they do not trust. Where there is no trust, there can be no effective leadership. Trust is earned over time. It cannot be conferred or demanded.

For leadership to happen, there must be followers. Followers can make or break the leader. As there are leaders who don't lead, there are followers who don't follow or who make leadership difficult or even impossible.

Followership, like leadership, must be learned. Good followership is not defined as following blindly. Good leaders do not demand that. A successful leader once told me, "The best subordinate is not one who always agrees with me—surely not one who always disagrees with me—but one who gives me the confidence that together we will not err."

Is leadership always learned, or are some born with it? In truth, it is both. Mature leaders do not suddenly appear out of nowhere. Some have more natural ability than others, but in the end, leadership skill, like swimming, cannot be learned by reading a book. It is learned by doing. Leadership is at its best under the most difficult circumstances.

When selecting a leader, beware of someone who:

- Is quick to flaunt power and take privilege for himself or herself;
- Resorts to intimidation and manipulation;
- Is superficial;
- Is arrogant and personally ambitious.

President Woodrow Wilson once said, "Every man who takes office in Washington either grows or swells." The same could be said of organizational leaders. They serve best by using servanthood techniques. Servant leaders are motivated not by power or prestige, but by genuinely putting the interests of others and the cause ahead of themselves, by enabling rather than enforcing. Such is the leadership that people follow willingly and with good results.

> **Servant leaders are motivated by putting the interests of others and the cause ahead of themselves.**

I recommend that everyone entrusted with leadership responsibilities, and everyone who reads this book and serves on a board of directors, reads a book on servant leadership every year.

No one said it better than the master teacher when instructing his disciples: "If any man desires to be first, the same shall be last of all and servant of all."

## DISCUSSION QUESTIONS

1. Do the directors of your board see themselves as leaders? The chairperson may be the first among equals, but all directors should look for opportunities to exert their influence in the wider community.
2. What style of leadership is modeled in your boardroom? Is it the gavel-wielding, bully pulpit sort, or is it servanthood leadership? Are you conscious that the leadership style exhibited in the boardroom is emulated throughout the organization?
3. Do your board members "follow" in ways that make leadership easier and more effective?

# CHAPTER 19

# Smelling Salts for Troubled Organizations

**W**hile some of you are trying to get your organizations into orbit, others are working to keep theirs from falling to the ground. Organizations are launched in a blaze of enthusiasm, but, like people, organizations have a life cycle. Some, as demonstrated in the biblical parable of the sower and the seeds, show great promise for a season but quickly wither and die. And thousands of nonprofits die each year. Others get renewed.

How do you go about resuscitating an organization that has gone flat and is staving off extinction? It can be done—it is being done—but it takes a strong will, some skill, and a measure of nerve.

## Define your purpose

Before going about the hard work of resuscitating an organization, satisfy yourself that it is worth saving. Times change. Some organizations have outlived their usefulness. They are no longer needed. They need to be allowed to die, maybe even helped to die.

Other organizations still have life and relevance, but they have fallen behind the quickly changing times. They are peddling yesterday's newspaper. Their renewal needs to begin by identifying a purpose that is relevant and urgent.

**Some organizations need to be allowed to die— maybe even helped to die.**

While engineers were working day and night to perfect a better typewriter, Bill Gates came along with the invention of the century that revolutionized how we communicate and do business worldwide. Those old typewriter companies, for all the good they did, had outlived their usefulness.

Some organizations are troubled precisely because they no longer have a defined sense of purpose. The would-be resuscitators' first challenge is to determine the signature purpose for which their organization exists. Is it consistent with what the members/constituents expect and what is within the organization's competence?

## Communicating your purpose

After you have identified your purpose, your reason for existence, consider how to communicate it in a compelling way. It is an essential part of building your new brand. A hospital or clinic should be seen as promoting health, not as a place where sick people come to die. Re-Uzit stores do not exist to dispose of middleclass leftovers. Their proceeds feed the hungry and restore lives.

If your organization is not pulsing with excitement, before you think the answer lies in a new multi-colored, glitzy brochure, look at the needs you are addressing and how you are presenting them to your public.

The Water Street Ministries in Lancaster, Pennsylvania was for years the place where homeless could find shelter and a warm meal on a cold night. They made modest appeals for contributions, but the general public was under the impression that things were all right. Then suddenly, or so it seemed, it was learned that they would need to reduce services due to a lack of funds. The public was surprised and responded with an outpouring that was beyond expectations. While doing a great job of ministry, the WSM had failed to keep the public well informed of its needs.

## It is all about people

Whether bringing a new organization into being or rejuvenating one that has fallen on hard times, people are always a large part of the solution. To echo Collins again, "Do you have the right people on the bus?" People are at the root of organizational decay, just as people are at the root of organizational renewal.

The people under whose direction a venture went flat are not likely to revive it. It is said, "If you do what you've always done, you will get what you've always gotten." To get improved results, you need some new thinking, and that is most likely to come from new people. Finding them can be a challenge, but the harder part may be to make room for them. That often involves parting with some who have served well but who are no longer what is needed now. Rotating them off the board so they can be succeeded is challenging but sometimes necessary.

> **To get improved results requires some new thinking, most likely from new people.**

## Qualifications for new directors

As you make room for some new directors, look for these qualifications and characteristics in the people you are hoping to find:

1. **Persons who know something.** The world is filled with people of goodwill, but goodwill alone won't cut it. You do not have time for on-the-job training. You need people who have demonstrated that they have the *skills* needed. All other considerations are secondary.

2. **Persons with a can-do attitude.** As there are introverts and extroverts, right-handers and south-paws, so there are persons who are naturally optimistic and courageous. God loves them, and caution has its place, but you cannot build or revive an organization with gloomy naysayers. By eternally fixing on obstacles and dangers, pessimists drain energy out of a system when it is most needed. You need to find directors who bring *positive energy* to your board.

   > You need to find directors who bring positive energy to your board.

   Negative people are like dragging brakes. Brakes have their place—I don't want a car without them—but if brakes do not release, they interfere and eventually burn out. Do not lose valuable time by trying to get positive results from negative people.

   I was a partner in a startup for-profit venture. The concept was exciting, but . . . . meeting after meeting, our efforts were going nowhere. We were on the verge of despair when good fortune came our way. The member who was continually looking on the dark side resigned. He was replaced by someone whose ideas were not always well thought through, but he was of a can-do nature. Our venture took off. Only in retrospect did we realize the burden of negativism.

3. **Persons with stature.** Few things will help you more with rebuilding your public image than someone with an already established reputation. It may be a challenge to recruit such persons, but on the other hand, persons with these skills are often looking for a challenge with long odds.

## Root out weaknesses or build on strengths

The reflex of many leaders of troubled organizations is to ask, "Where are the problems?" Their assumption is that if they can identify the problems, they can find a solution. Maybe.

## Sometimes the better approach is to build on strengths

Even in troubled organizations, there are usually strengths to build on. Finding them is the challenge. One way of doing that is through a method known as Appreciative Inquiry (AI). Instead of looking at problems and deficiencies, AI shifts the focus to strengths and successes. Negatives feed on negatives and produce negative results. Inversely, a positive line of reasoning is more likely to produce positive results. AI has the ability to change how people think, and as a result, it can transform the outlook.

There is some wisdom in the old proverb, "Things are not as good as they seem when they are good and not as bad as they seem when they are bad." That is to say, there is good even when things appear to be bad. AI says, find it and build on it. Let good drive out the bad.

## Set goals

Regardless of what approaches you use, mile markers are needed to measure progress. Some boards are reluctant to set goals for fear of not achieving them. But boards that fail to set challenging yet attainable goals, complete with intermediate markers, get discouraged because they have no way of tracking progress. Nothing succeeds like success, so it is said, and so it is.

Ventures that refuse to set goals by which progress can be measured may live with an illusion of progress. Or they may get discouraged because they have no way of tracking how well they are doing. Whether measured against performances of others of like kind, or your own previous accomplishments, you need some way to track progress or the lack of it.

## Don't lose your nerve

There will be days when you will question if you are going to make it or if it is worth the effort. A famous organizational expert has said, "At the midway point, all ventures appear doomed." Put your shoulder to the wheel and push. Invite others to support the effort.

Remember, you are not working to restore something to its former glory days. They are forever past. You are working to invent a new future for your revived organization.

Many organizations that have fallen on hard times can be renewed—if they deserve it, if they still have a purpose. I have seen it happen. I have participated in helping it happen. Up from the ashes. It begins with people—people with competencies and a can-do spirit. People who set goals for themselves, and then passionately move heaven and earth in their fulfillment.

**Boards that fail to set goals get discouraged.**

**When it appeared that London would succumb to Germany's relentless bombing, Winston Churchill gave a speech that consisted of just five words. Putting his cigar aside for the moment, he surveyed his audience. Then slowly and deliberately he said, "Never, never, never give up." He repeated it twice more and sat down. Speech finished. Point made!**

# DISCUSSION QUESTIONS

1. Is your organization facing challenges? If so, does it deserve to be resuscitated, or has it served its purpose?
2. What are the strengths and assets to build on, including staff?
3. Can the needed turn-about be achieved with present personnel, or are changes necessary?
4. How do you want the organization you are resuscitating to look when you are finished? What will it be doing?
5. Have you reduced what you want to accomplish into a plan with specific goals, including mile markers to achieve them?

# CHAPTER 20

# Spirituality in the Boardroom—Beyond Seeing

I n their private lives directors are doers. They are lineal thinkers who know how to get practical results. Is that not what organizations are all about?

Could it be, I ask rhetorically, that in all our drivenness, while we are fixated on plans and policies, budgets and best practices, something very important is eluding us? Might there be important topics that never get on our crowded agendas or dashboards?

When we will reflect on our board work with the benefit of hindsight, will we conclude with the Indian poet, "The song I came to sing is unsung. I spent my life stringing and unstringing my instrument."

God made us body, mind, and spirit. We go to great length to train our minds and care for our bodies, and it is right that we should. But spirit? How does that enter into our worldview? And what does it have to contribute to this discussion of board effectiveness? Is that not a Sunday topic, reserved for the church or synagogue? Let's look a little deeper.

## Beyond seeing

We are joined in our virtual discussion by Alfred Lord Tennyson who in his poem *In Memoriam* reminds us–

Our little systems have their day;
They have their day and cease to be:
They are but broken lights of thee,
And thou, Oh Lord, art more than they.

The Apostle Paul says much the same: ". . . .so we fix our eyes not on what is seen, but on what is unseen, since what is seen is temporary, but what is unseen is eternal." II Corinthians 4:18 (NIV).

This casts the focus well beyond our long-range plans and budgets, beyond what can be seen, and introduces a transcendental dimension. I will discuss it in two parts: personal spirituality and spirituality within the organization.

## Personal spirituality

In Chapter 1 I said, "Apart from people, an organization is only an empty shell. It knows nothing. It can do nothing. It is people who imbue an organization with greatness." The spiritual dimension enters our discussion, therefore, through the people who are in it, whether as directors or employees. From where else could it come?

Spirituality is seen as the outworking in real life of a person's religious faith. It is weaving what we each believe into the fabric of our life, and it shapes our ethos. It defines what we value and how we use authority. It influences how we live.

Spirituality is a very personal and complex subject that is beyond the scope of this chapter, and my ability to do it justice. A wealth of literature is available on the subject of personal spirituality, and we can do little more than introduce the topic here. Suffice it to say, however, that spirituality should not be confused with religion, nor should religion be confused with one's particular church. Spirit is essence. It has a supernatural, mystical quality that supersedes human understanding. It is at the same time part of human experience, whether recognized or not. It adds a third dimension to our board service, as well as to our personal lives.

Persons of *Christian* faith exercise a transcendental relationship with God through prayer and seek Divine guidance and blessing. Witnessing a stunning sunrise or sunset, listening to a bird concert in a forest, or enjoying a performance of Handel's Messiah can also be spiritual experiences. They enrich the soul and add beauty to our lives.

However incomplete this discussion of *personal* spirituality may be, and however you experience it, spirituality enters the boardroom through the spirituality of the people who are in the room.

## Spirituality in an organization

In their book *Awakening Corporate Soul*, Eric Klein and John Izzo state that organizational leaders need to do more than fixate on the balance sheet, team-building, or annual plans. They suggest that the solution for satisfaction and success is to create an atmosphere that feeds whole human beings, including the inner person.

How do directors go about creating a spiritual atmosphere for something so amorphous, even so mystical, in an organizational setting? How does spirituality influence boardroom behavior and decision-making?

William A. Guillory, in *The Living Organization*, suggests what others have discovered, that "Organizations are at their best when spiritual principles are combined with best practices."

Robert Greenleaf, that Quaker AT&T executive who popularized servanthood leadership, writes about leaders needing to know the unknowable and foresee the unforeseen. We hear persons in positions of authority say that they are driven to their knees, seeking Divine help with their difficult decisions.

Before I offer some practical suggestions for how the spiritual dimension can enrich our board work, a few thoughts about how the Bible might relate to this discussion.

Many of us grew up with a theology that separates the secular from the spiritual. Work and worship, word and deed were as separate as night and day. This is, most Biblical scholars agree, a false and unfortunate separation, and yet it persists and distracts from the richness with which we should view our work.

This wrongheaded theology needs to be replaced with the recognition that God is with us in the boardroom as God is with us in our places of worship. The main difference is that God's presence is recognized in the latter and too seldom in the former.

God is with us in the everyday as God is with us on the Sabbath. To feed the hungry, to teach the illiterate to read, to give shelter to the homeless, and yes, to give direction to an organization doing worthwhile things, can be regarded as an exercise that fulfills our Christian calling, when done in that spirit and for that purpose. God is in the boardroom.

With that in mind, I offer the following practical ways in which spirituality can be expressed in the boardroom.

1. When we bow our proud heads to recognize a higher power we become changed people. Assertive egos and know-it-all personalities, which can be so disruptive to boardroom dynamics, are replaced with a spirit of mutual respect and humility. A good spirit can supersede bad boardroom procedure and behavior. But good boardroom procedure can never compensate for a bad spirit. Spiritual atrophy is often a precursor of disunity and arrogance.

2. Spirituality lays the foundation for morality and ethical behavior. This is not meant to imply that secular boards are less ethical. To the contrary, I have known some that were more ethical than some that make this profession. I mean only to suggest that Christian teachings are at the root of a faith-based organization and help to

define its ethics, so poignantly summarized in Christ's Sermon on the Mount (Matthew 5–7).

3. Waiting on God or, if you prefer, waiting on the Spirit, however you want to refer to the transcendent, brings an otherness into the equation. It is an antidote to the myopia and narcissism that pervades our world. Directors who allow for a third dimension in their decision-making are more likely to search for the unseen and prepare for it. They are more likely to ask, "What if?" To read what is between the lines. To ask, what might our metrics be missing?

4. Consciously recognizing God's presence in the boardroom and in our lives changes the attitude from "We are in charge," to one of service in a greater cause. It recognizes that God owns the vineyard; we tend it. A hymn states it beautifully: "The work is thine, oh, Christ, our Lord, the cause for which we stand. And being thine will overcome its foes on every hand."

This is by no means an exhaustive list. You are invited to add to it out of your own experience. Many of you already begin your meetings with a meditation of some sort. Some pause for a moment of silent prayer before voting on an important decision. The challenge is to build on these sacred moments until the entire meeting takes place within an awareness of God's presence. "Waiting on God" takes discipline when the agenda is full, as they always are.

Spirituality must, however, never be seen as a substitute for best practices or performance.

It is not an end in itself. It informs and enables. Nor is it a guarantee for success. I know of no research that suggests that faith-based organizations have a lower failure rate. We know that their meetings can be as ruckus as any.

In *Setting the Agenda: Meditations for the Organization's Soul*, Rick Stiffney and I acknowledge that "Humans are more likely to experience this world [of spirituality] when they have exhausted their intelligence and allow themselves to enter the world of unknowing, where the peace of God 'surpasses all understanding' (Philippians 4:7)."

Stiffney and I go on to observe, too, that "a new flowering of the Spirit awakens our consciousness and floods our souls with energy and enthusiasm. It liberates us from being captivated by that which will one day disappear. It helps us reach beyond ourselves. It tames our assertive egos and narcissistic tendencies and gives us joyful hearts to serve others."

## Seeing what cannot be seen

Our deeper answers may not come by lengthening our workday, by working harder or even smarter, or by finding yet another way to cram more into a busy day. Our better answer may be in slowing down and enjoying the laughter of children at play, by watching birds building their nests or a squirrel burying a nut for a mid-winter snack. It may be in tuning out the noise with which we are all surrounded and, in the stillness, getting in touch with something deeper inside of our souls.

Directors ought to care for their souls as they care for their bodies and minds. They should bring that consciousness with them to their board work. Doing so can be transformative both for the director and the organization.

## QUESTIONS FOR DISCUSSION

1. Does your board consciously nurture a spiritual dimension in its work?
2. Do you think of your organization as having a soul, a spiritual dimension? Do you nurture that?
3. Do you consciously invite God's spirit to guide you in your planning and decision-making?
4. Do you think of your board service as being part of your Christian vocation?

# CHAPTER 21

# Under the Shadow of Litigation

It seems so contradictory and so just plain wrong that something as noble as service on a nonprofit board should be subject to personal liability, but such is the case in our litigious society.

It is appropriate that directors of publicly funded nonprofits should be held to a reasonable standard of care. The public needs to be protected against unscrupulous persons who roam the earth and, on occasion, infiltrate even nonprofit organizations.

How can directors protect themselves and the organizations they represent against legal liability? Directors are, after all, removed from the day-to-day operations. How can they be held responsible for something that goes wrong? The standard that must be met, and against which director liability is judged, is simply what, in legal language, is called a "reasonable standard of care." Consistently and conscientiously abiding by best practices, in both governance and management, goes a long way toward complying with this requirement. This includes the following in practical terms:

1. That the board meets regularly and discharges its fiduciary role faithfully in an open and responsible manner. If that is not how the board on which you serve is conducting itself, and if you are powerless to change it as an individual director, you may consider resigning from the board to escape liability or damage to your reputation.
2. That management be mandated to abide by all applicable laws and regulations, with monitoring to ensure that it is happening. Directors may not understand the fine points of the law, but at a minimum they must not knowingly and recklessly violate laws and regulations.
3. That the organization requires "truth in advertising." Do not purport in public utterances to be doing what you are not doing.
4. That the board engages a competent auditor to review the finances and cash management practices annually and makes sure that any recommendations are followed.

## Transgressions that may result in liability

The most common transgressions resulting in legal action are employment related. A board is responsible to put in place policies that prevent violations, including these especially vulnerable areas:

1. **Discrimination in hiring and promotion, and wrongful discharge**. Courts and the general public have become very sensitive to matters related to race, gender, and age discrimination. Even apart from the law, matters of discrimination should be of concern to directors. Even an unproven accusation can be damaging to an organization's reputation.
2. **Sexual harassment**. Directors are expected to require management to maintain a safe work environment, including appropriate sexual

harassment policies and training, and to monitor that the organization is in compliance.

3. **Complete due diligence in hiring.** In simple language, know whom you are hiring onto your staff. At a minimum, get references, check the police report, and do a Google search.

4. **Conflict of interest.** Directors who find themselves with a dual interest—e.g., employing a close relative, or leasing or selling a property to the organization on whose board you serve—should recuse themselves from voting on such issues, and this should be recorded in the minutes.

Special care should be exercised, and perhaps legal counsel should be engaged, when an organization is contemplating a merger and/or when substantial governmental contracts are in place or under consideration. This applies especially to how such discussions and decisions are recorded in the board meeting minutes.

> **Special care should be exercised, and perhaps legal counsel should be engaged, when an organization is contemplating a merger and/or when substantial governmental contracts are in place or under consideration.**

## Managing director liability

Director liability can be managed through procedures that many organizations already have in place:

1. A bylaw provision that shifts liability from the director personally to the nonprofit, excluding, however, anything of a fraudulent nature.

2. A Directors and Officers Liability Insurance policy purchased by the organization that indemnifies a director or officer against wrongdoing. D&O policies are subject to limits and a deductible and apply

to both defense of a suit and judgments. The defense provision may prove to be especially beneficial, as most claims are settled out of court.

3. Some homeowner policies maintained by directors personally also have limited coverage against D&O claims.

4. Board policies that require management to:

- Maintain a grievance procedure;
- Conduct annual employment reviews that document where performance may be lacking, along with the opportunity to bring performance up to a reasonable standard;
- Perform due process before discharging an employee.

The bottom line in director litigation is contained in what is referred to as the "Business Judgment Rule":

Even where a corporate action has proven to be unwise or unsuccessful, a director will generally be protected from liability arising therefrom if he or she acted in good faith, and in a manner reasonably believed to be in the corporation's best interest, and with independent and informed judgment.

As always, "Prevention is better than cure."

Directors and officers should not be paranoid, but neither should they be naive about the liability they assume as directors. This liability can be managed by the conscientious, consistent application of best practices outlined in this chapter.

## DISCUSSION QUESTIONS

1. Does your board meet the "reasonable standard of care" test? What about the "Business Judgment Rule"?

2. Do you have policies and practices in place that prevent and/or lessen director liability? For example, do you perform due diligence before making major decisions? Do you avoid conflict of interest? Do you have grievance procedures in place?

3. Does your board have a bylaw provision that shifts director liability from the directors to the organization?

4. Do you have Directors and Officers Liability Insurance? Should you? If not, are you prepared to assume that risk, however large or small?

# CHAPTER 22

# Lighten Up—A Place for Humor and Celebration

**M**any boards, if rated on a scale of joyfulness, would rank somewhere just above a gathering of morticians. Board work is, to be sure, serious business, but must we be so glum? Are there no occasions for humor or celebration?

## A place for humor

Humor can be a lubricant that relieves tension and helps to focus an issue. A former chairman of Mennonite Central Committee had a knack for telling a short, timely story when things got tense. To conclude a long, inconclusive

> I heard that someone walked by a room where we were having a meeting. Not knowing what was going on behind closed doors, he asked, "What is going on in that room?" When he was told it was a board meeting, he said, "Impossible—they were laughing."

discussion that not everyone thought was worth the time it was taking, he told about a boy who was banished to his room for refusing to eat a dish of prunes. While standing at his window watching a lightning storm in progress, and not knowing that he was being observed, the boy was heard to mutter under his breath, "Such a fuss over a few prunes." It served to relieve the tension in the room and move the meeting along.

> **Humor can be a lubricant that relieves tension and helps to focus an issue.**

Then there is the story that Abe Lincoln reportedly told while presiding over a raucous meeting of his Union Army generals. In his apocryphal story, a boy was lost in the woods on a dark night while a major thunderstorm was in process. In desperation, he prayed, "If it is all the same to you, God, I would prefer a little less noise and a little more light." Lincoln made his point.

Humor is different from telling jokes. Humor sees the lighter side of an issue. Most sarcasm is not humor. It is biting criticism that feeds negativism, although it may not be entirely pointless. Humor is at its best when it is not caustic or used at the expense of others.

> **Humor sees the lighter side of an issue.**

If you are fortunate to have someone in your ranks who can lighten the atmosphere without being obnoxious or too time-consuming, consider yourself fortunate. Humor has its place, even in the boardroom.

## Board service should be fun

Maybe not every moment of every meeting is fun, so perhaps *satisfying* would be a better choice of words. A poorly conducted meeting that goes on forever without a worthwhile conclusion can try the patience of a saint. But board service does not need to be that way. It can also be deeply satisfying, as we serve with people who, like ourselves, are donating their time and treasure on behalf of a worthy cause. Service is a privilege, not a sacrifice. Truly, it is in giving that we receive.

> **Service is a privilege, not a sacrifice.**

Service is payback time for many. Our generation has been blessed like few before us—a few wars not withstanding—and arguably like none after us. Muhammad Ali states it so poignantly, "Service to others is the rent we pay for space we occupy." Let's do it with joy!

But we enjoy service only when we do it well, when we can see something accomplished, when we see lives changed. If you are not enjoying your board service, perhaps you should consider releasing your position to someone who will.

## Celebrating

While writing my concluding chairman's report for the board of American Leprosy Missions, I found myself enumerating our accomplishments and concluded each with, "Something to celebrate." Then it struck me. We had never celebrated. I was embarrassed and determined to make up for lost time.

Upon arriving in Greenville the evening before our quarterly meeting, I asked senior staff to help me make room on the agenda for a celebration. They looked at me incredulously. Did I not realize how full the agenda was?

"I know, I know. We'll cut the evening session a little short, and then we'll celebrate into the night," I said. Looking into their doubtful faces, I asked, "What had you planned for our dessert following the evening meal?" "Cake?" Excellent—could we keep that for our celebration? Are there any candles around?"

Diane was softening up and volunteered, "There's a closetful left over from a fundraiser." Then she volunteered to get some balloons and streamers. Chris got into the spirit and offered a favorite celebratory CD. On short notice, I asked Carol to emcee the event.

We recessed the evening board session at a record hour. The directors descended the stairs apprehensively. Quickly, their mood was transformed by the sound of lively music. Balloons and streamers came into view. For a moment, we stood around silently and somewhat awkwardly. Then Carol picked things up with some appropriate remarks, followed by more awkward silence. Clearly, we did not know how to celebrate!

Feeling some obligation to dispel the anxiety, I stepped forward hesitantly. After selecting a candle from the table I lit it somewhat nervously and, facing the group, I held it high and said, "Here is to the memory of Mike who served us so faithfully as treasurer and whose friendship we miss."

The ice had been broken. One after another the directors and senior staff came forward to light a candle and offer a celebration. We forgot about time as everyone joined in. At the end of the evening, our table of lighted candles looked like an altar, causing some to inquire where the fire extinguisher was located. While the directors mingled over coffee and cake, some were heard to say, "We must do this again—soon!"

Budget for the event? Maybe $10. It ranks among the most cost-effective board activities ever.

Celebrate! Look for excuses to celebrate. Celebrate an anniversary, a fundraising success, a year of accomplishments, a birthday, a retirement, a major staff appointment. It will add a joyful dimension that will make your board work go better and give you more to celebrate.

> **Look for excuses to celebrate.**

## DISCUSSION QUESTIONS

1. Are your meetings joyful or heavy?
2. When is the last time you celebrated?
3. What could you plan to celebrate now? An anniversary? A fundraising success? Employees who have completed 10 years of service? A director who is retiring?

# CHAPTER 23

# Ending Well

"For everything there is a season. A time to be born and a time to die." "A time to engage and a time to disengage," to paraphrase Solomon.

After having invested ourselves in a cause, whether as an employee or as a director, we want—and we deserve—to leave with a sense of satisfaction, of being appreciated. Sadly, that does not always happen. The pain of termination sometimes overshadows years of devoted service. Instead of feeling appreciated, retirees sometimes end up feeling pushed aside, discarded. Few dynamics are more difficult to manage than when an invitation to service expires before the officeholder is ready to relinquish the office.

As in other parts of life, retirement needs to be addressed further upstream. Many boards do not manage expectations well. They allow directors or senior employees to subconsciously conclude that the office belongs to them for life. Anything less seems hurtful and

**Retirement needs to be addressed further upstream.**

potentially disruptive. This atmosphere can be avoided or at least reduced. Here are some suggestions.

## Term limits

I have concluded with some ambivalence that term limits are the best of imperfect options. They are admittedly arbitrary and sometimes result in losing the services of someone you would dearly like to retain. They are, nevertheless, in my opinion, better than the alternative. They not only set the stage for rotation, they serve notice that the officeholder has a limited window of time within which to make his or her contribution.

My preference for a maximum length of service on a board is somewhere between six and nine years, divided into terms, as you prefer. I have reservations about the practice of bringing retired directors back after a year of absence, restarting the clock. With rare exceptions, directors have contributed what they have to offer within the first six or nine years. The organization will benefit more from new blood.

**Term limits are the best of imperfect options.**

## Criteria for re-upping

Re-upping (continuing service) should not be assumed. It must be earned by performance. Organizations should adopt performance criteria by which incumbent directors qualify to succeed themselves. Anything less builds mediocrity or worse into an organization at the highest level. Determining who qualifies or who does not qualify to re-up can be so excruciatingly difficult as to make term limits appealing.

The procedure by which incumbent directors are re-upped should demonstrate in the presence of all that the invitation to continued service is extended with the anticipation of *future* service, not as a reward for *past* service.

A forward-looking board should never find itself in a position where a mediocre director is re-upped because no candidates are available to succeed her or him. Sometimes those responsible to nominate successors (often the Board Service Committee) are only too willing to allow an underperforming director to continue just to have a warm body in each chair. This underscores the need to have a list of vetted and qualified directors ready to step in.

Leaving the board properly after a term(s) of service has a lot to do with leaving at the right time. Some directors hang on for one term too long. They are only too ready to hear fellow directors tell them patronizingly, if not always honestly, "You will be missed." So they re-up for another term. Leaving a board can be likened to playing a game. You should quit while it is still fun. Let that be a balancing thought, not a rush to the exit.

> **Leaving properly has a lot to do with leaving at the proper time.**

## Post-service contact

A recently retired director once said of a board on which we had both served, "When you leave that board, it is as though it never was." How unfortunate. How unwise. Retired directors are loyal supporters. They should not be allowed to go from being at the very center of the organization to disappear into oblivion.

Some boards share board meeting minutes with retired directors for a year after their retirement. This softens the loss inherent in retirement. Some have an emeritus category for a very select group of retirees. Such an honor should be for a specified period and not for life.

The Mennonite Economic Development Association has on occasion made room in their schedule to honor and hear from former directors. It is a kind of deferred thank you that also pays good dividends through continued moral and financial support. It just makes good sense.

## Ending well

The responsibility of planning for a good retirement falls to both the organization and the retiree. I am acquainted with an organization that includes the following phrase in its board service covenant: ". . . to step aside graciously and with goodwill to my successors and the cause when the time comes." This suggests that retirees, too, must participate by managing their emotions and expectations by embracing retirement in a positive spirit.

I am pleased to say that while my transition into retirement was not easy, these post-retirement years have been among my best. There is life after retirement. (What makes it so is the subject for another day.)

The importance of leaving right was brought home to me when a Mennonite Central Committee service worker had an emotional breakdown, requiring her to return to the United States for treatment. She responded well, but we were taken aback when her therapist recommended that she be permitted to return to her overseas location so she could "leave right." Leave right? Did the therapist not know or did he not care that this involved the purchase of an expensive airline ticket for traveling halfway around the world? Almost against our better judgment, we allowed ourselves to be convinced. It was done, and in retrospect, I conclude that we did only what was due her.

After giving of ourselves to serve a cause in which we believe, we want and deserve one more thing. That is to leave on a good note. To end well. May it be so for all of us.

# DISCUSSION QUESTIONS

1. How does your board manage director expectations to avoid bad endings?
2. Is it understood that re-upping is by invitation and based on performance? That it is not the incumbent director's prerogative?
3. How do you recognize or reward board service rendered?
4. How do you maintain contact with retiring directors?

# Afterword

**Y**our reading of *Doing Good Better* has no doubt affirmed many of the good things you are already doing. Congratulations. Continue to do them. They provide you with a foundation to further improve your boardmanship.

You may also have discovered areas where improvement is possible. Think of them as opportunities for growth. The ideas presented in this book need to be adapted for your particular use. Feel free to do so. But before putting this book back on the shelf, I suggest drawing up two lists, addressed to yourself:

1. Ways I can improve *my* board performance in the next year. Be specific. Identify one, two, or three personal goals for the year—ways to improve your performance as a director. State them in writing and review them throughout the year. At the end of the year, make another list. This is how directors grow through mediocrity to greatness. Be all you can be—for yourself and the cause you serve.

2. Ways our *board* could increase its effectiveness in the next year. Here, too, be specific, but also be wise in how you present your suggests to your fellow directors in a nonthreatening way. This

will be a test of your boardmanship. Be prepared to listen, but be persistent in your pursuit of excellence.

It is a noble thing to serve others. Both giver and recipient are blessed. Service enriches the soul and makes the world a better place. My highest hope is that reading this book will help you in your efforts of **Doing Good Better**—and will ensure that you enjoy it more.

# Board Self-Assessment Form

**KEY**

| A | B | C | D | E |
|---|---|---|---|---|
| Strongly agree | Agree | Disagree | Strongly disagree | I don't know |

## Board membership

1. We have in our board membership the whole range of skills needed to do our work.  Ⓐ Ⓑ Ⓒ Ⓓ Ⓔ

2. Our board is representative of the membership or constituency in matters of gender, race, geographic region, and religious diversity.  Ⓐ Ⓑ Ⓒ Ⓓ Ⓔ

3. All members of our board are dedicated to the cause and support it with their time, talent, and money.  Ⓐ Ⓑ Ⓒ Ⓓ Ⓔ

4. We have a Board Service Committee that leads the board in a self-assessment exercise annually and provides nominees as needed to keep our board strong.  Ⓐ Ⓑ Ⓒ Ⓓ Ⓔ

Comments: _____

_____

_____

## Board duties

1. We are clear on the purpose for which we exist (vision and mission).  Ⓐ Ⓑ Ⓒ Ⓓ Ⓔ

2. We have a clear plan and long-range strategy to fulfill our purpose with measurable goals.  Ⓐ Ⓑ Ⓒ Ⓓ Ⓔ

3. Implementation of our plan has been delegated to management or committees with appropriate instructions and policies.  Ⓐ Ⓑ Ⓒ Ⓓ Ⓔ

4. The financial and personnel resources needed to complete the plans are reasonably assumed to be available.  Ⓐ Ⓑ Ⓒ Ⓓ Ⓔ

5. We evaluate program-effectiveness annually with management.  Ⓐ Ⓑ Ⓒ Ⓓ Ⓔ

6. We keep our members or constituency well informed.  Ⓐ Ⓑ Ⓒ Ⓓ Ⓔ

Comments: _____

_____

_____

## Board committees

1. We have the right board committees and are well served by them.  Ⓐ Ⓑ Ⓒ Ⓓ Ⓔ

2. Our committees have clear job descriptions and complement the work of the board.  Ⓐ Ⓑ Ⓒ Ⓓ Ⓔ

3. I serve on the _____  Ⓐ Ⓑ Ⓒ Ⓓ Ⓔ
   _____ Committee(s).

4. The committee(s) on which I serve are serving a  Ⓐ Ⓑ Ⓒ Ⓓ Ⓔ
   necessary board function well.

5. Is there another committee on which you would  Ⓐ Ⓑ Ⓒ Ⓓ Ⓔ
   prefer to serve?

Comments: _____

_____

_____

## Board meetings

1. Our meetings are orderly and productive.  Ⓐ Ⓑ Ⓒ Ⓓ Ⓔ

2. The board meeting attendance record is good.  Ⓐ Ⓑ Ⓒ Ⓓ Ⓔ

3. The agenda distributes the available time well,  Ⓐ Ⓑ Ⓒ Ⓓ Ⓔ
   including time for visioning.

4. The frequency and length of our meetings is  Ⓐ Ⓑ Ⓒ Ⓓ Ⓔ
   about right.

5. Our board works in a harmonious atmosphere  Ⓐ Ⓑ Ⓒ Ⓓ Ⓔ
   that allows for vigorous exchange.

6. Action items are well processed and presented in  Ⓐ Ⓑ Ⓒ Ⓓ Ⓔ
   proposal form.

7. Our meeting docket gives us the information  Ⓐ Ⓑ Ⓒ Ⓓ Ⓔ
   needed to do our board work.

8. The minutes accurately record what transpires at  Ⓐ Ⓑ Ⓒ Ⓓ Ⓔ
   our board meetings.

Comments: _____

_____

_____

## Relationship between board and CEO

1. The relationship between the board and CEO is characterized by trust and mutual respect. [A][B][C][D][E]

2. Our CEO has a clear job description. [A][B][C][D][E]

3. The board reviews its relationship with the CEO annually. [A][B][C][D][E]

4. The board supplies the CEO with guidance and support without interference. [A][B][C][D][E]

5. The CEO supplies the board with the information needed to do its work. [A][B][C][D][E]

Comments: _____

_____

_____

## Legal/financial

1. We have a budget with midyear reporting that permits comparisons. [A][B][C][D][E]

2. We have a bylaw provision that protects directors against directors and officers liability. [A][B][C][D][E]

3. We have an independent financial audit annually with follow-up as necessary. [A][B][C][D][E]

Comments: _____

_____

_____

## Overall board rating of its governance performance

Use a 10-point system with 10 being the highest.  Ⓐ Ⓑ Ⓒ Ⓓ Ⓔ

Comments/suggestions for commendation and/or improvement:

_____

_____

_____

_____

_____

_____

Name                                                    Date

# CEO Annual Review Outline

Since the appointment of the CEO is a board's single most important decision, servicing this relationship is of utmost importance. An essential part of servicing the CEO/board relationship is the annual review. I suggest a two-way *conversation*, in contrast to a performance appraisal, in which the CEO is more of an object than a conversation partner.

The board chairperson, to whom the CEO is responsible, conducts the review with another director present to increase objectivity (perhaps the Board Service Committee chairperson).

## Pre-review checklist

1. Inform the CEO of your intention to initiate a review. Do not take her/him by surprise.
2. Review the job description. What is the CEO expected to do?
3. Review the written summaries of previous reviews.

4. Invite comments from the board in an executive session in advance.
5. Invite comments from senior staff who report to the CEO, to get a general sense of the rapport that the CEO has with staff. Be careful not to undercut the CEO. Do not show agreement or disapproval with information they volunteer. The key is to *listen*.

## The review

Schedule the review in a comfortable setting. Reserve a minimum of 90 minutes, free of interruptions.

Make some effort to put the CEO at ease. Remember, you want a positive outcome.

1. Invite the CEO to reflect on the past year, noting the following:
   - Highlights;
   - Disappointments;
   - Staff support;
   - Relationship with the board;
   - Level of satisfaction in the position.
2. Next, the board chairperson reflects on the past year, noting especially matters related to the CEO's performance. This *must* include both commendation and areas in which improvement is needed. Do it constructively, thoughtfully, sensitively. Invite response. Be interactive. A secure CEO will welcome such a review and see it as an opportunity to improve performance and relationships, if approached appropriately.
3. Show personal interest in the CEO, but respect his or her privacy. You might make a general inquiry about the following and allow the CEO to decide at what depth to respond. Do not interrogate.
   - Kids;
   - Hobbies;

- Health (maybe inquire when he or she last had a physical examination);
- Plans for a leave or studies to upgrade skills;
- Future plans. If thought is being given to retirement or termination, this should be a subject of open discussion.
4. Reserve some time to anticipate—to dream together—about what the next year will require by way of executive leadership. Identify priorities and challenges you anticipate. Allow or invite the CEO to share goals he or she has for the coming year.

## Post review

Prepare a written summary of the review, covering both affirmations and areas where adjustments are needed. This summary can be hard to write and must catch the necessary nuances, but it is a necessary part of the exercise. Conclude the summary by giving the CEO an opportunity to add his or her own statement, after which the written exchange is shared with the board in executive session and kept in a confidential file.

**A qualifier:** When the relationship between the board and the CEO is stable, a 360-degree review, such as the one described here, may be done every other year, with a more abbreviated conversation in the alternate year. My former boss used to warn against pulling the potato up too often to see how the spuds are growing.

**Annual salary review:** Some boards combine the salary review with the annual review while others separate them. It can be done either way, but one way or another, a salary review should happen annually. Organizations that are unable to pay a prevailing wage should not additionally compound the issue by leaving their CEOs feeling taken for granted or left dangling. Genuine care and thoughtfulness transcend salary, although the salary must allow a reasonable standard of living if the relationship is to continue.

If all of this seems like heavy work, it is. But it is an essential part of an enduring and productive working relationship between the board and its CEO.

**EXHIBIT C**

# Director Self-Assessment Form

Name_____ Year elected_____

| Ⓐ | Ⓑ | Ⓒ | Ⓓ | Ⓔ |
|---|---|---|---|---|
| Strongly agree | Agree | Disagree | Strongly disagree | I don't know |

Rating (Add comment as desired)

1. Our board meetings are well conducted and worthwhile.     Ⓐ Ⓑ Ⓒ Ⓓ Ⓔ

2. I regularly prepare for and attend board and committee meetings.     Ⓐ Ⓑ Ⓒ Ⓓ Ⓔ

3. In its deliberations, the board is consciously aware of our stated vision, mission, and goals. Ⓐ Ⓑ Ⓒ Ⓓ Ⓔ

4. Our board understands the division of function between governance and management as illustrated in the Big X (see page 7), and does not get bogged down in operational detail. Ⓐ Ⓑ Ⓒ Ⓓ Ⓔ

5. Issues requiring board action are presented in proposal form and facilitate decision-making. Ⓐ Ⓑ Ⓒ Ⓓ Ⓔ

6. I enjoy my service on the _____ Committee(s) and feel we are making a worthwhile contribution.

7. I would like to be considered for the following office or committee appointment:

    _____

    _____

8. All things considered, I think our board is doing an excellent job. Ⓐ Ⓑ Ⓒ Ⓓ Ⓔ

9. I enjoy my service on this board and am willing to continue serving with joy. Ⓐ Ⓑ Ⓒ Ⓓ Ⓔ

10. Suggestions for how my service on this board could be used more effectively:

    _____

    _____

_____  _____

Name                                                      Date

# CEO Search Checklist

The appointment of the CEO is one of the most important decisions a board makes, since all of its operational decisions flow from or through that office. The board may invite comment from the departing CEO, but it is basically on its own in making this important decision. It is wise to keep the goodwill of the departing CEO to make the ensuing transition easier. The following are some suggestions about how to proceed:

1. Appoint a Search Committee. I suggest three members but not more than five. If the board is very inexperienced with searches, consideration might be given to inviting a professional HR person, who is not a director but a friend of the cause, to serve as a consultant.
2. Draw up a job description that states the duties assigned to the position, along with the desired outcomes.
3. Draw up the terms and qualifications:
   - Educational requirements
   - Values

- Experience/demonstrated competencies
- Salary range depending on qualifications and benefits

4. Announce the position and invite candidates. Throw the net wide.

5. The Search Committee evaluates the applicants against the stated terms and qualifications and selects three to be placed on the short list. Those selected are vetted thoroughly, including the following, as seems appropriate:
   - Police background check
   - Credit rating
   - Church/pastor reference
   - Previous employment references (subject to prior approval by the applicant)
   - Personal interview with the committee, including the board chairperson (see suggestions below)
   - Other testing as seems advisable

6. The Search Committee makes its selection. It invites the candidate to meet members of the board and senior staff in person in a semiformal setting(s) to further check compatibility preliminary to a formal recommendation. The chairperson of the Search Committee should be present for these meetings.

7. If the lights are green, the Search Committee consummates the understanding with the candidate and presents him or her to the board for appointment. Assuming the vote is favorable, the candidate is then announced and installed. If the Search Committee candidate is not confirmed, the Search Committee reopens the selection process. I recommend not more than two weeks overlap with the outgoing CEO.

8. The unsuccessful candidates are thanked.

9. The Search Committee is thanked and dismissed.

## Suggestions for the Search Committee

1. Organize yourselves before the interview. Demonstrate some professionalism by having your questions well organized. Remember, you, too, are being observed by the candidate. My preference is for the committee to agree on the questions in advance, and then have the chairperson of the Search Committee carry the conversation. Schedule some time between appointments so you have the opportunity to check signals with each other, and so candidates don't run into each other.

2. Invite the candidates to tell a bit about themselves. Listen for information, but even more, look for personality characteristics. Observe personal warmth or lack of it. Observe evidence of self-confidence or lack of it. Check for arrogance. Ask about books they have read, vacations they have taken. What are their hobbies? Allow them to present themselves as they are. Make an effort to make them comfortable.

3. Ask open-ended questions that pertain to the competencies needed to fulfill the job description and that are experience based, not hypothetical. For example, have them tell about a fundraising success they participated in. Ask them to tell about a major project they administered and how they handled an underperforming employee. This is not an entry-level position. A CEO must be able to hit the ground running.

4. Some committees use a spreadsheet that lists the traits required to fulfill the job description. After each interview, each member of the Search Committee assigns a value to each candidate. If there are five traits you are evaluating, you may assign twenty points to each (for a total of one hundred points), or if one trait is of greater importance, you could assign it forty points and spread the remaining sixty points over the other four traits. In the end, all the scores are tallied and available to influence the final

selection. If major questions remain, do not hesitate to request a second interview.

5. Remember, you must limit your questions to job-related qualifications. You are not permitted to ask personal questions about religion, marital status, age, etc.

# Writing Effective Proposals

A board should require committees and management to present in proposal form all issues on which action is expected. This procedure helps to facilitate board meetings and results in better decisions.

A proposal summarizes the main elements of an issue and recommends a course of action. It should state:

- The issue being addressed—in one or two paragraphs;
- The action desired. Is this for information and/or discussion and/or for a decision?
- The background considerations supporting your conclusion. In several paragraphs state: How will it be paid for? Will additional staff be required? Are there space considerations? Does this have the support of other departments implicated by the action proposed? Will there be a review date? Answer questions before they are asked.
- The recommendation you are asking the board to approve.

The written proposal should not exceed one page in length, although it may have attachments as necessary. It should be distributed in advance of the meeting where it will be acted on.

Staff proposals should be presented to the board by the CEO, or minimally with her/his approval, without exception.

The board has four options: (1) approve the recommendation as presented; (2) amend it; (3) table it for additional information; or (4) vote it down. Proposal writers know they have hit the bull's-eye when a proposal is approved by the board and read right into the minutes. Be clear, however, that the board is not obligated to approve a recommendation.

Even as writing proposals must be learned, so boards also must learn how to evaluate a proposal on its merit and not redo all the work that has preceded its presentation. The board must resist the ever-present temptation to engage in meaningless wordsmithing. After a reasonable time for discussion, the board should decide in favor of one of the four options offered above. Discussion should not be allowed to go on ad infinitum.

The board action should be recorded in the board minutes, and the proposal added as an attachment.

# Governance Guidelines: A Model for Start-Ups

1. Introduction: The _____ (insert name of organization) is committed to working in compliance with all applicable laws and regulations, as well as its own bylaws.
2. Board responsibility: The Board of Directors (BOD) can and will delegate functions, but the responsibility for what does or does not happen rests with the BOD.
3. Meeting attendance: Directors are expected to attend all board and committee meetings. When unable to attend a meeting, directors are expected to ask to be excused. Two consecutive unexcused absences constitute disqualification from the board.
4. Meetings: Directors are expected to read materials distributed in advance. In meetings, they are expected to address and interact with each other in a respectful manner. This applies also (especially!) to disagreements. Routine business will be transacted

by consent. Meetings will be conducted according to *Robert's Rules of Order,* as adapted for use in a smaller assembly.

5. Agenda: Board meeting agendas are prepared jointly by the chairperson and CEO and distributed in advance.

6. Meeting frequency: The _____ (organization name) BOD will meet quarterly. The chairperson and the secretary may call additional meetings as the need arises. It is expected that the chairperson and the CEO may meet between meetings of the board as necessary.

7. Reporting: The CEO will keep the BOD well informed through written reports and otherwise as necessary. Written reports will be shared with the BOD at least one week before the regular meeting.

8. Payment: Directors serve gratis. Expenses related to meeting attendance or assignments are reimbursable.

9. Confidentiality: The _____ (organization name) BOD is committed to doing its business in an atmosphere of trust and openness. Where confidentiality is required, directors pledge to uphold it conscientiously.

10. Conflict of interest: Directors are expected to recuse themselves from participating with items in which they have conflicting interests.

11. Use of committees: _____ (organization name) BOD operates from a principle of board wholeness. Committees may be used for special assignments and/or to prepare issues for action by the BOD. Committees have only the authority given to them by the board. Committees shall prepare and promptly distribute a record of their meetings.

12. Evaluation: The BOD will perform a self-assessment and a relationship review with the CEO annually. Program evaluation will be part of the annual planning process.

13. Policies: The _____ (organization name) BOD is committed to doing its work, as much as is practical, from a policy perspective. It will create a board policy manual where all board policies will be filed and kept readily available for consultation. The responsibility for updating this manual annually is assigned to the secretary of the BOD, working with the CEO.

14. Recommendations or written proposals: Major issues needing board action shall be presented in recommendation or proposal form. This applies both to management and to board committees.

15. It is understood that service on this board is by election or invitation. Retiring directors agree to relinquish their office with goodwill to their successors.

After approval by the board, these guidelines will be included in the proposed policy manual.

# About the Author

Edgar Stoesz has spent most of his adult life in a variety of for-profit and nonprofit organizations, most of them in a faith tradition. After his retirement from thirty-five years in six administrative positions with Mennonite Central Committee, he served on and chaired the boards of Habitat for Humanity International, American Leprosy Missions, and Hospital Albert Schweitzer (Haiti). He also chaired the board of Heifer Project, served as Moderator of the Atlantic Coast Conference of Mennonite Church USA, and served on the executive committee of Mennonite Economic Development Associates.

Edgar is the author or co-author of twelve books, five of which are related to board work. Among them is the widely acclaimed book, *Doing Good Better*, first published in 1994. He has written numerous articles and addressed or conducted workshops for more than 150 boards.

A native of Mountain Lake, Minnesota, Edgar resides in Akron, Pennsylvania. He and his late wife, Gladys, have four grown children and seven grandchildren.

# *Doing Good Better*
# ORDER FORM

If you would like to order multiple copies of **Doing Good Better** by Edgar Stoesz for groups you know or are a part of, please email:

**bookorders@skyhorsepublishing.com**
or fax order to **(212) 643-6819**.
(Discounts apply only for more than one copy.)

Photocopy this page and the next as often as you like.

---

### *The following discounts apply:*

| | |
|---|---|
| 1 copy | $11.99 |
| 2–5 copies | $10.79 each (a 10% discount) |
| 6–10 copies | $10.19 each (a 15% discount) |
| 11–20 copies | $9.59 each (a 20% discount) |

*Prices subject to change.*

---

*Quantity*                          *Price*      *Total*

_____ copies of **Doing Good Better** @ _____  _____

Shipping & Handling (add 10%; $3.00 minimum) _____

TOTAL _____

# METHOD OF PAYMENT

❐    Check or Money Order
         (*payable to **Skyhorse Publishing** in U.S. funds*)

❐    Please charge my:
      ❐ MasterCard   ❐ Visa
      ❐ Discover     ❐ American Express

\# _____

Exp. date and sec. code _____

Signature _____

Name _____

Address _____

City _____

State _____

Zip _____

Phone _____

Email _____


SHIP TO: (if different)
Name _____

Address _____

City _____

State _____

Zip _____

Call: (212) 643-6816
Fax: (212) 643-6819
Email: bookorders@skyhorsepublishing.com
(do not email credit card info)